BIRDS FROM WOO

Birds from Wood

Making decoys and other birds

Hugh O'Neill

The Crowood Press

First published in 2000 by
The Crowood Press Ltd
Ramsbury, Marlborough
Wiltshire SN8 2HR

British Library Cataloguing-in-Publication Data
A catalogue record for this book is available from the British Library.

ISBN 1 86126 253 1

Artworks by Cy Baker.

Photograph previous page: An antique of unknown date. This prized Pintail, typical of working decoys of a couple of centuries ago, is from the small collection held in the offices of the las Tablas de Damiel wetland reserve just north east of Ciudad Real in central southern Spain.

Typeset by Textype, Cambridge
Printed and bound in China by Dah Hua Printing Press Co. Ltd

CONTENTS

PREFACE

This is a book of limitless horizons! Its initial focus is upon carving and painting ducks – what were known at one time as 'decoys'. Early man, concerned only with survival, made bird representations to use as lures to help fill the pot. Possibly after a particularly good day's hunting he may have carved a bird as a gift for a partner or child, but the history and development of bird carving is very firmly rooted in the making of decoys.

It is only in comparatively recent times, when man had more leisure, that we saw bird carving develop into a creative and artistic pursuit in its own right.

So although the focus of the book is on ducks, I soon found that in drawing together the material there was a need to delve into other areas, so several of the pictures used to illustrate techniques are of other birds – as indeed are many of the text references. Almost everybody likes ducks; and the natural interest soon spreads over into waders. My own all-time favourite bird is the Curlew – not only because of its beautiful shape and the ethereal sound of its cry but because I so love the Curlew's natural habitat.

Many people have a particular interest in raptors and birds of prey – I also share this. Those who prefer their art/craft in smaller packages may well look to garden and woodland birds. My own carving vision is not confined to ducks and waders, but also takes in owls and hawks. The fact that I do not also fashion swans and geese may be just because you have got to stop somewhere. And stopping somewhere does become a problem when you enter this field; the horizons really are boundless.

Of course you have to be interested in wood. It is not just a block of material that has to be knocked into the shape that you need. To get the best out of it you have to understand it; love the feel of it; know about its varieties, and which variety is the best to use for a particular purpose. The more you know about wood, the better will be your carving; and you will soon become interested in exploring different woods and working out how you can best exhibit the figuring, the colours and qualities of the wood. Wood itself can become a fixation – a lifetime's pursuit of knowledge and experiences. Or maybe it will not matter what wood you use because you will choose to cover it with paint.

You may start with a simple stylized approach to decorating your carvings. Your aim may be to produce your own versions of the type of painted ducks seen in gift shops today. Most are imported from China, cost only a few pounds, and are very popular. The simplistic style of painting is not challenging but can still look effective and quite attractive. However, you will probably not wish to stop there. The next stage is a painted stylized representation of feather patterns – usually executed in artist's acrylic colours.

The highest art of the bird carver's world are the wholly realistic carved and painted life-sized birds that win competitions and which may well be priced at over a thousand pounds. It is not unusual for such competitions to be judged by ornithologists who look for a feather-perfect representation of the real thing. Prize-winning birds of this quality demonstrate craftsmanship of a sublime level and one that takes many years of practice to fully achieve. You also need to be a bird physiologist to enter this field! There are an increasing number of people who have substantial collections of work of this nature.

If you develop an understanding of colours and brushwork you are half way to painting pictures of birds. Doing two-dimensional paintings of birds (and feathers) has made me a better painter of three-dimensional birds, and vice versa. Then again, field sketching can be one of the inputs into the carving process. Field observation expands your understanding of birds enormously, and becomes essential if you want to move into the realm of dynamic carvings such as birds in flight or 'displaying' – that is, stretching their wings or fanning their tails – preening or feeding.

So, now you have become not only an artist, but also a twitcher! One minute it is the occasional welly-clad visit to a hide in the marshes; and the next it is a camera and binocular-draped visit to Greenland or Lake Baikal.

And, of course, even on the Sunday stroll in the park, you will carry a camera. You have to become a photographer. Or do you? There are books of plans; there are countless books of pictures. You do not *have* to do it *all* yourself. But it is difficult not to get sucked into this too. The books of plans are all very well, but soon you want to produce something that is original and very quickly you can get into cameras, lenses, films, emulsions and filters. Sometime ago I found that my 'input' pictures were themselves in demand and I sold more mounted photographs at craft fairs than I did finished birds.

In outlining some of the avenues and potential horizons we have, of course, walked straight past such issues as developing a love of the habitats of our models. You can not just look at the birds, but at the whole ecosystem in which they live. Many times you visit an area with a vague hope that you will get a distant glimpse of a particular bird. What you have really gone for is the sheer joy of walking and exploring the countryside – wild moor, crag, estuary and marsh (and a good pub lunch).

Oh! and there is one more avenue. I know that for me it is just around the corner. It must be possible to take an image – say a photo, and turn it into a scale plan using computer graphics. I have already found out that with computers the moment you start to follow a particular area of use you get hooked!

And I nearly forgot. You may even get drawn into something else. Taking your work to craft fairs can be fun with a new circle of friends (fellow crafts people), and a little spare time income.

So, we are going to to dip or delve into many of these aspects. At each stage the book will present you with choices. It will say that you can do it this way – but if you do, you will have to understand about cameras, paints, woods and so on. Or you can simply go to the library, take out a book and copy a plan. You might even go to a shop, buy a ready 'carved' bird and paint it. The choice is yours.

THE DECOY DUCK

We all started as hunter-gatherers. Today, although the need is reduced, many of us still have strong hunter urges; and most of us are pleasured (or plagued) by the drive to gather – or to collect!

Man is unique within the animal kingdom for two ongoing instincts. The first is the drive to create things of beauty for their own sake, and the second to improve and develop the things around us (both natural and man-made). To us little is perfect and not much is good enough to be simply left alone. Of course we do not always get the 'improvements' right, and what one person sees as a development, another sees as an abomination. We get to a very old age before we feel 'Yes, that will do; that's OK', and at that stage we want to freeze it – capture it and retain that bit of perfection for ourselves and for posterity. So we photograph or draw it, paint it or carve it; and then frame it or stick it on the mantelpiece. Or of course give it to a loved one.

It does not matter what it is, but we constantly strive to improve the functionality, efficiency and/or the aesthetic appearance of everything – from ourselves and our own skills to our environment – and this pattern of behaviour can be traced back to the very early days of man. Take our furniture, or at least, one item of it – the chair. All it needs is a support which holds us in the right position for sitting, and that is sufficiently padded to be comfortable. In all our houses we have such chairs – probably the utilitarian pieces we have in the kitchen. So why do we need luxuriously upholstered easy chairs or the exquisitely shaped and carved chairs of Chippendale and Sheraton?

We see these same drives in the development of the Decoy Duck. Their very existence stemmed from the desire of early man to improve hunting performance as providers. Over the years decoys have been 'developed'. Functional decoys are now made of plastic. They are lifelike and float well with their moulded factory manufacture; they are so cheap that it is not worth the hunter's while to carve their own; and they will even withstand the impact of the odd stray shot. Yet there are competitions where dedicated craftsmen compete with others to produce superb, carved wood, and totally life-like birds that even float naturalistically. Their beauty, realism, and the skill of the carver quite take your breath away. The fact that the decoys are seen 'in competition' is itself interesting – once a human being is dedicated to excellence, they want to test their skills against others. Competitions provide a yardstick by which the individual can test their own ability levels.

So where did it all start, and what caused us to turn the making of an essentially utilitarian item into an art form?

Of course man, even back in hunter-gatherer days, took scraps of driftwood or soft stone and fashioned them into decorative artefacts. Today, bird carvings are just one of a vast range of arts or crafts that we practise. Many carvings are stylized relying on beauty of line or a display of the character of the material. They are now original 'art' – not just a mere copy of the real thing. With decoys, the hunter's quest for realism developed only much later into an art form.

The early hunter quickly identified that their quarry had certain behaviour patterns and that these patterns could be turned against their prey. One of the most important of these is that ducks 'gather' where there is a supply of food. Foreshores quickly fill up on an ebbing tide. Passing birds need to be 'told' that there is food below. A piece of water remains empty for some time, then one or two birds will come speculatively, three or four more will follow. Eventually there will be enough feeding birds to indicate to others passing by that the water is safe and that there is clearly something worthwhile investigating, and whole flocks settle. The increasing number of birds gathering on a piece of water now becomes exponential. So the hunter wishes to show passing birds that the water is safe. Early Egyptians are known to have tethered live birds in areas within range of their nets.

Nobody knows when the first artificial birds – 'decoys' – were used. The first archaeological evidence came in 1924 when a basketful of eleven decoys was found in Lovelock cave in Nevada. The birds were of Indian origin and have been dated to over a thousand years old. They were substantially made of reed and had wing feathers of real birds tied over the main part of the body. Some even had the skins of birds tied on. They broadly imitated the Canvasback duck with white body feathers and black 'painted' heads, necks and breasts. Why they were in the cave is a matter of speculation. They may have been left for later collection by a hunter who failed to return; or may have been a part of some funereal ritual. Certainly at the time that these ducks were made there were Indian tribes in the area whose lives were improved by several

sophisticated developments including fresh-water leats to the villages and channelled irrigation of their crops. The tribes had developed from hunter-gatherers to agrarian communities; once they made that transition they were well on the way to starting to organize and 'improve' things.

The name decoy came into the English language from the Dutch. Its root was 'de kooi', the Dutch for a cage or trap.

In about 1650 teams of Dutch drainage engineers were employed in East Anglia to drain some of the marshes that made up the Fens. Not only did these teams bring with them land reclamation skills, but they were also very proficient at harvesting wildfowl. In the margins of a suitable piece of water they would build their *de kooi*. These were long, funnel-shaped tunnels known as 'pipes' and were made of interlaced withes and nets. The birds would be enticed into the large open mouth of the funnel often by trained dogs known as 'pipers'. The ducks would see the dog, often a water spaniel, playing down inside the pipe and their curiosity would overcome their caution. So the ducks would enter and the dog would then move deeper into the ever-narrowing tunnel. The hunters would be hidden but would emerge once the ducks had passed them – effectively sealing the escape route. Eventually the ducks would reach a point where they could be taken out by hand.

Often the pond or lake would have a whole series of pipes each oriented in a different direction. The hunters could then use those pipes where they would be downwind of the birds. One of the earliest known pipes still exists. It is at Borough Fen in Cambridgeshire and it was in continuous use from 1670 when it was built right up to the latter part of the twentieth century.

Today the pipe is operated by the

Wildfowl and Wetland Trust on a farm near Peakirk, but now it is used so that birds may be caught for ringing.

Obviously from the early days part of the luring process was to first attract the birds to the water and then into the trap; the *de kooi* lure was augmented by the use of birds. Sometimes live domestic birds were used as in Egypt and elsewhere, but carved artificial ducks were much more convenient – and were less likely to be trapped and have their necks wrung in the half light of the evening hunt.

At about the time that the Dutch were working in East Anglia, the first settlers were crossing the Atlantic. Of course the Pilgrim Fathers came from the area near the Fens and, although it is not recorded, they may have taken *de kooi* ideas with them. On the other hand they will have found that the concept of using artificial lures – floating decoys – was already in place in parts of their new homeland. The widespread American practice of using decoys is now believed to have been that of the local Indians and not Dutch-based. During the early years of disease and famine the local Indians were extremely helpful to the settlers, and contributed their skills and local knowledge to joint hunting parties.

From here on in this brief history we will be focusing upon America; for the growth, and the excesses, of hunting, particularly commercial hunting, really happened there. Certainly the development of the decoy duck, and its eventual emergence as a collectable art form were primarily based there and really only came back into the UK in the second half of the nineteenth century.

In the early days of settlement, elaborately constructed pipes and traps were not really necessary. On America's eastern seaboard there was abundant game for the taking. A few crudely made decoys were useful, but not essential. The accounts of the first settlers around the Chesapeake area of the wildlife and game they found there are almost unbelievable to us today.

So, the hunters would carve and colour their own simple hunting decoys. No doubt the conversation around the camp-fire and later at the local tavern would get round to hunting successes and to the effectiveness of a particular style of decoy.

Many developments over the next couple of centuries have a bearing upon our story. Some came gradually, others were quite precipitate. Originally the relatively few hunters that there were were primarily concerned with filling their own pots, and possibly those of a few local friends. There were certainly more than enough birds to go round. Of course individual hunters would still try to improve their own decoys, for that is the way of man.

Then the demand for game started to rise and eventually the hotels and restaurants of the great cities of eastern America were calling for huge quantities. Rail transportation meant that birds shot one day could be on the table in New York next day, or even on the same day in Boston and Philadelphia. Commercial hunting became an important local industry.

The depletion in the bird flocks soon became apparent, hastened by the improving skills in luring and shooting. One development that the hunters turned to was the idea of rigs of floating decoys – sometimes as many as 100 or more. Weapons also changed; long, large-bore fowling pieces and punt guns could kill scores of birds at a single firing. Often a hunter would return from a day in the marshes with two or three hundred birds – ducks, geese and swans – sometimes with only one or two firings of their mini 'cannons'.

But man's constant striving for

improvement and growth does have a cost. Natural resources are only sustainable to a certain point, and the inevitable ill effects of over-use or abuse can only be tolerated to a certain level. Eventually, often too late, somebody will cry 'Enough – this is sustainable – but no more!' But by then some of the damage is irreparable; sometimes even the measures necessary to effect a partial repair are 'unacceptable' to the public.

By the beginning of the twentieth century output was exceeding input. Some species had already been hunted to complete extinction, others were getting perilously close to that. Today in Europe, there is indiscriminate shooting of wild birds, large and small for sport as much as for the pot; this, coupled with our changing agricultural practices, is also putting many of our wild species in danger of extinction. In 1918 the Americans decided that action was necessary and Congress passed the Migratory Bird Act which put an end to 'market hunting'.

But on the way, as market hunting increased year by year, many commercial hunters were spawned. These individuals were only interested in quantity kills and getting the product to market. They certainly did not mess about carving their own decoys.

A demand for good, realistic decoys now existed, and it was met: professional decoy carvers came onto the scene. Their primary output was working birds – ones that would float well, look right, withstand all sorts of rough handling, be repairable when shot; and in general be what we would today call of marketable quality.

Again tavern talk would identify some carvers' work as being more effective than others, and certainly some birds did look better than others. There was definitely competition amongst the suppliers.

Of course not all hunters were commercial killers. Hunting and shooting had long been a popular sport amongst a very wide cross-section of the community. At one end would be those primarily concerned with the day's shooting and with filling their own pots in the process. At the other, probably more wealthy end, would be those who enjoyed the entire hunting process and, like all hobbyists, would indulge themselves by investing heavily in their sport. They bought the best guns, the most expensive clothes, and certainly had their decoys carved by the best-known carvers. It was not long before wealthy hunters (and particularly those nearing the age of hanging up their guns) started to collect decoys.

With the passing of the Migratory Bird Act, however, the demand for working decoys fell right away. It was now only the hobby hunter who bought regularly, and it was only those professional makers who had already been identified by the

Not quite a decoy! A 'realistic' French Partridge carved and painted by Judith Nicoll, one of the UK's top bird carvers.

collecting market who still made a living.

When making for wealthy hunters and collectors you can no longer get away with the approach that anything will do as long as it looks reasonable. So quality improved – it needed to if the carver was to survive. Once you get into a rising quality market there are those who wish to move way ahead of the competition, so new techniques start to emerge and some old techniques are improved out of all recognition. Two movements became noticeable. One was impressionistic and largely followed the traditional approaches to decoy carving. This led on to stylized shapes and broad swathes of colour. In this same group were those who developed techniques for giving painted impressions of feathers that only followed the general form of the bird being represented – a technique that is now known as 'Featherstroke Painting'.

The other development moved increasingly towards total realism. Every individual feather is suggested, the colour is discreet and natural, and you often have to look very closely to assure yourself that it is not a real living or stuffed bird.

Over the years something else had happened. Different makers had, naturally, developed their own styles. The keen collector now had to have an example of each style and the work of each of the top carvers. Other collectors went more for work representing the styles of a particular region.

Guilds and local groups of people interested in the subject of decoys have formed. Most of the members are makers, but there are also collector groups. Through such gatherings and conventions, competitions developed. On both sides of the Atlantic there are now local, national, and international competitions and exhibitions for the various styles of carved and/or painted birds.

What started as a hunting aid and therefore focused upon ducks and geese also broadened its vision and now encompasses all forms of birds. If you go to an exhibition today you will see birds of every type. Owls feature as widely as ducks, geese are regularly seen as is the occasional swan. Hedgerow and garden birds abound, and hawks are widely favoured. There are very few carvers in the UK who stick with only one species, and even in America there are today few who only make ducks. One factor that is clearly rooted in the working origins of carved birds is that of size. A few carvers of raptors and birds of prey make birds that are scaled down in size, but in general the vast majority of bird carvings that can be seen in exhibitions today will be lifesized.

In the UK there are as yet only a few collectors while in the States there are a considerable number. All this is reflected in prices. At the bottom end of the market a collector can build up a display of the painted, scaled-down ducks from China which may only cost from £5–20. For a polished wood stylized bird you may be asked anything from £50 upwards. Life sized stylized painted birds are frequently in the £75 to £200 mark, but when you move into the realistic painted birds the prices will range from £500 to £5,000 and more.

In America where prices for most things are cheaper than in England, the picture is very different. Craft work generally is better valued. The English prices can almost always be at least doubled. Some of the top carvers can command $20,000–30,000 and at auction important antique decoys have made double those figures.

WORKING DECOYS

These, as the name implies, are designed for use, that is to lure wildfowl to within shooting range. Since they are made for use in water they must float upright and at

A flock of birds. At the back are two stuffed birds used as models. The Curlew is a simple 'polished wood' carving in Sycamore. Along the front are three 'feather carved' pyrographed ducks; a simple painted 'slick' Carolina Wood Duck, and a 'Featherstroke' painted Redhead.

the correct height. Of course they must look like a duck, but not necessarily of the type you expect to lure. They must be capable of withstanding the rigours of use. In competitions for carvers they would be judged on such criteria. They are likely to be smooth (that is, not have feather patterns carved on); they are unlikely to be brightly coloured (in fact many are antiqued) and the colour is usually in broad, flat patches with no feather simulation; they could be hollow, and they are likely to be weighted – they may even have a metal keel to keep them upright and reduce wind drift.

There are also working decoys, usually of wader species, that are intended for seashore work. These usually have a long single leg – often a single dowel – for sticking into the mud. Today some twitchers use decoys – particularly wader decoys – to entice birds into camera range.

DECORATIVE DECOYS

These are intended to be only decorative, and are unlikely to ever be used for hunting. They closely follow similar criteria to working decoys except that they are not weighted. They may have some incised feather carving but are often smooth in which case they are classified as *slicks*. A subset of the decorative decoy has stylized feather patterns painted on. Often the feathers are impressionistic and one particular style of painting we will be examining is known as *featherstroke painted.*

WOOD CARVED

Here we are moving away from the realms of decoys or bird simulation and into pure wood carving. The piece may be a simplified representation of the shape and size of the real bird or it could be stylized and even to some extent abstract. They are obviously intended to be purely decorative and much of their appeal is usually that they display the beauty of the figure and the colour of the natural wood from which they are carved. The finish may be oiled, polished or varnished.

STAINED DECOYS

These really are a hybrid, but the style is sufficiently popular to be separately identified. Their increasing popularity has been given stimulus by the availability of the wonderful range of wood dyes that have now come onto the market. Often birds in this category look very like antique working decoys, but because it is a stain and not an opaque paint that has been used to decorate, the wood figure usually shows through.

FEATHER BURNT

Again this is not really a distinct category but it is important. In the process of carving a realistic decoy each feather is exactly or impressionistically carved into the surface. Some feathers are undercut so that they stand proud. One of the ways of producing this detail is to first carve the outlines and then to burn on the detail, including each barb of each feather using a pyrograph (hot wire) tool. The result is a bird that is quite realistic, the brown colouring of the burnt wood closely resembling the drab colour of many hen

birds. Some carvers regard this as being the finished stage and do not go on to paint the actual feathers. I must acknowledge that this is my own favourite style.

REALISTIC DECOYS (BIRDS)

Here sufficient feathers are carved on, or the surface is textured, to look like a live feathered bird. They are then painted with a number of layers of thin wash. The colour always matches the hue and tone of the colours on the real bird. Being applied in multiple thin washes the paint does not clog the lines of the carving so both the shape and the colour of the

The Glad Eye. These glass eyes for ducks, waders, hawks and owls are obtainable from taxidermists' suppliers.

feathers of the real bird are reproduced. At five feet, and even closer, it is difficult to see whether the bird is real or not.

As we will see there are several approaches to the incising of the feathers on birds that are to be realistically painted. Some are achieved very quickly, others take a hundred or more hours per bird.

It is worth noting before we pass on to the techniques of tackling any of these styles of carving that there are some traditions that you may wish to observe. In the competitions in the States some of these 'traditions' have become competition rule requirements. There, even totally realistic decoys may have to meet a floating test. They have to sit at the correct height in the water and this will be tested by the judges. This probably means that the body has to be hollow and that lead plug weights have to be inserted. It is an old tradition that hollow bodies should have a loose pebble inside them, so that you can then tell that they are hollow by rattling them.

Obviously cast pewter legs (a great boon when carving a standing wader) are not allowed. They have to be made of wire covered in a mouldable and carveable material. The only 'artificial' element allowed in these extreme competitions are the glass eyes.

— 2 —

FIRST FIND YOUR BIRD

The urge to carve their first bird comes to people in different ways. Some, probably already dabbling in woodwork, have a particular love for a certain species and decide to try to carve one. Others just like the idea and wonder what bird to start with. Some go to an exhibition or competition and are so impressed by the realism of what they see that they decide to 'have a go', and they then look around to see what bird to start with. In fact I started when thinking about something that could be worked in wood to 'demonstrate' while idling away some empty hours at the craft fairs where I was selling some of my woodturning. I soon found carving a much more challenging and interesting occupation, so today I carve rather than turn. And, of course, everybody loves ducks!

Whatever the motivation all come up against the question 'Where and with what do I start?', and it is here that there are so many avenues open to you. You certainly need plans – and *a plan*!

I am one of those kinds of people that when I get a new interest I spend hours in bookshops and end up buying a book or two. This first search yielded (not too quickly) one or two books with full-scale accurate and detailed working drawings. There were also a number of books with 'plans' for ducks, raptors and birds of prey, but in which the drawings were not to any particular scale and were often simplistic in their representations.

One of the country's greatest bird carvers and painters, Judith Nicoll, told me that some carvers have to work from ornithological books which have pictures and very tiny silhouettes of the bird in flight. She also said 'Some, like me, work from stuffed birds. Others are really adventurous and go out into the wilds with cameras or sketch-book in order to produce their own plans.' I, like many others, eventually ended up trying all these routes.

In your early days of carving you will probably need drawings in all three planes – Plan (top view); Elevation (side view or profile) and Front View or Section(s). As you do more carving you will find that the need for accurate, three-plane plans, begins to lessen. Eventually your perceptual and spatial abilities will have developed and you will have acquired a reasonable understanding of bird physiology and behaviour. Now you have reached the stage of being able to take a single picture and to carve a good three-dimensional representation. Certainly, the books of full-size plans provide the easiest entry point, and although nearly all of us start there, there comes a time when most carvers want to move on.

In the bibliography at the back of this volume some useful source books are detailed. In fact the literature focusing upon decoys is prolific – there is much less on the carving of other species. A few of the decoy books are excellent. The drawings are good and the detail accurate. Several of the American books, however, have sketchy plans for a species of bird that is often bigger than its UK equivalent. In some, the outlines are lumpy and poorly detailed. Many of the drawings give

Bird carvers soon build up a library of books of plans and bird references. The open book by Pauline McGowan is extremely useful.

only the minimum of feather detailing, some none at all. There are also a number of books with fairly accurate drawings but these are scaled down to a third, a quarter or one-sixth of the real size.

As you will see from the bibliography there is also a range of books which detail the techniques of carving birds. There are few which focus upon natural-finish *wood carved* pieces; some are mainly concerned with decorated *slicks*; and some do go on to look at *realistic* decoys. There are very few that are particularly good on painting birds.

Most of the books only provide drawings for birds in simple positions such as sitting on the ground, with head erect and

straight forward. You very quickly want to go beyond that. It is at this stage that you will probably decide to produce your own plans and might consider fieldwork and the use of a camera.

What is in particularly short supply are books that provide large, accurate colour pictures that clearly show feather arrangements and colours. A good source for these are the wildlife magazines (particularly those of the BBC) as they now have superb colour photographs.

If you ever get into the realms of entering competitions or exhibiting you will find a real need for accurate information on the details of features and feather arrangements. You will be surprised at the level of knowledge of judges and visitors and at the accuracy that they demand, even in a stylized carving. So you too will probably end up as a twitcher with a sketchbook and pencil. Some of you may eventually move on even further to enter the realms of watercolour and oil painting.

As a side issue, few of the books listed say much about types of wood (or about the very basics of whittling and carving). There is a reason for this. Early carvers used whatever came to hand. A lot was done in pine because it is buoyant and there was always plenty locally. Once carvers became more interested in incising detail they looked for softer, more carveable woods. In North America it is now taken for granted that you will be using native Basswood or imported Jelutong.

Most American carver/authors also assume that today your work will be done with high-speed burrs, so who needs to know about the use of knife or chisel? On the other hand, some of our more traditional woodworkers do not recognize this as being 'carving' at all! I, myself, use a little of everything.

Initially the choice of where you start has really been made for you – by the birds that have been drawn in the good plans book that you have bought. You start with those that are easiest and when you find that you are well pleased with the results, you will then choose the more complex poses. You will however soon have worked through the really good reliable plans and be into scaling up outline drawings and refining the detail. For this you will also be looking at bird books and nature magazines for good pictures or illustrations so that you can draw into the outline your own detailed feather patterns. Then one day you think 'Oh! I would like to carve a . . . .(in my case a Kite)' and there are no plans or drawings available. You have now reached the stage where you need to photograph, or even to sketch birds in the wild and then go back to the studio to draw these up into your own full-size plans.

I had already been something of a keen photographer for many years by the time that I began to move from woodturning into the carving of birds. Although I was not then interested in twitching, my wife Eve and I do enjoy wild places – mountain, moor and fen. So, looking for birds that I would like to carve, we made many journeys to bird sanctuaries and spent hours in hides snapping everything that came into sight.

About this time, Eve had to make a long rail trip across the Canadian prairies to a Physio congress in Winnipeg; she took a camera with her. She was enchanted by the thousands of Gophers that she saw, and took many feet of film from the slow-moving train. When she came back and had the films processed there were scores of pictures of the limitless but seemingly empty prairie. On just a few frames, with the aid of a very powerful magnifying glass you could see some tiny light-coloured dots. 'There!' she said proudly, 'Those are Gophers'. Our duck pictures from those early days of bird watching soon became

known as 'Gopher Pix'!

After some months of twitching – that we greatly enjoyed – we knew a lot more about waterfowl behaviour and how they looked when flying, landing and floating; but there really weren't any pictures from which you could produce carving plans.

Then, one Sunday, we had a family outing into central London. It was a lovely spring day so we went into St James Park to see the flowers. We enjoyed the tulips and daffodils for half an hour and then went to the pond. There they were, ducks aplenty of every shape, size and description. They came right to our feet and I'll swear that they even posed – plan, elevation and full frontal! Four reels of film later I had the basis of a good library. Indeed many of the pictures that we took that sunny afternoon have since been sold as mounted prints. Some months later, on another Sunday afternoon at the pond in Regent's Park I completed the collection.

Just as a point of interest, we have since visited the Wildfowl Trust reserves at Walney and Slimbridge. They are good sources for 'behaviour' pictures of indigenous bird species, but the ducks there have not been quite so well trained and although they come close they do not swim right up to your feet – and pose!

So, what photographic equipment is required if you are going to build your own picture library? You need at least one long-focus lens. They are useful even in St James's. This generally means a 35mm single lens reflex camera. If you go for larger formats even a moderate telephoto lens requires a re-mortgage!

Working from hides puts you straight into the 1000mm plus league. There I found that I had to use a 500mm mirror lens which is fixed at f8, and mount this on a 2 or 3 times magnifier. There were two problems. First the effective aperture was reduced to about f22 meaning very slow shutter speeds. Secondly the weight

A Widgeon. In St James's Park the birds come to your feet – and pose!

and slow speed makes a very heavy and rigid tripod essential. All this becomes quite unwieldy in a small hide. And even with this the images were really too small to be useful.

It was all so much easier at the Park. Most of my best pictures were taken on a fully automatic camera with a 28–75mm zoom lens, (now) using Kodak Gold Ultra ASA 400 print film. Only occasionally is the lens switched to a 75–200mm zoom. One day I might be able to afford one of the latest 28–300mm aspheric zoom lenses! There is always a polarizing filter on the lens as this allows me to modify the colour of the background water.

So a trip to the London parks enormously reduced the need for expensive super-zoom photo equipment, and a good day can produce a lifetime's supply of good models. One keen bird-watching friend has a relatively simple 35mm single lens reflex camera and can couple this to his twitcher's monocular telescope. Another friend does quite well using a video camera with vast magnification potential (I think it is a 40 times zoom). He then extracts single frames on a computer-linked editor, feeds them into Adobe Photoshop software, further blows them up, plays around with background and picture enhancement, and finally

A Tufted Duck on Regent's Park lake. Here they are not quite as friendly as at St James's.

prints them out on A4 paper on a photo real Epson printer. But then he understands these things!

I no longer do any processing. Since abandoning transparencies, my print films are now mailed to a Kodak service.

Of course I could have stuck to books of pre-drawn plans, but I find that going to the park, the nature reserves and the marshes has given me a feel and a depth of understanding that I could never have got from books. Certainly it is only on field trips that you see those important behaviour patterns and natural 'poses' that can be turned into a unique carving.

There is something else that field trips give you. You do not need waders and waterproofs since you are only going to take a walk along a river bank or lakeside.

An important input into duck carving is to have a collection of feathers. So whenever you see a feather lying on the ground pick it up, slip it into a plastic folder and take it home. We will later be talking about painting feathers – not just painting feathers onto carved birds, but making reference paintings of single feathers. I now believe that doing this is an essential part of the development of the skills needed to make realistic bird carvings.

A moment ago I mentioned a friend's video set-up. There is no doubt that photography is in the middle of a sea change. In fact it is already difficult to sell second-hand enlargers, because of the huge swing in the domestic and serious photographer markets to digital cameras and computer-processed printing. Even

21

without a digital camera a computer can be very useful. 7 × 5in colour prints are an ideal starting point. They are all that is needed to give guidance on feather detail when you get round to the carving and painting stage; but they can also be used as the basis for drawing full-sized plans.

Using even a simple black and white hand scanner the images can be fed into a computer where they are processed into line drawings. According to the software that you use you may only get an outline, although many programs will also reproduce the more prominent feather patterns.

Interestingly the software need not cost a fortune. I do now have Adobe Photoshop, which is brilliant, but there are many good lower-priced packages. The one that I found the most useful was also the cheapest! Serif Photo Plus has a sequence which is described in their manual as 'Edge Detection'. Using this you can convert a colour print into a charcoal drawing. In fact the program has a 'Charcoal Drawing' button which will do the whole conversion process for you with one press of the button, but the results are not always quite as good as going through the various steps one at a time increasing or decreasing settings as you go. The output is a set of A4 pages with clear but light outlines with key detail lightly showing. The next stage is to strengthen the line with a black Biro or fine-point felt-tip pen (see page 96).

With the best equipment that most of us are ever likely to have access to, the drawings produced at this stage are unlikely to be full-sized.

The simplest method of scaling up can be a photocopier. All you need is access to, and skill in using an enlarging photocopier. Here you first work out the required percentage increase in size you need to take your line outline up to a lifesized drawing and dial the percentage increase into the copier. Provided the full size will fit onto A3 paper you are OK,

however I find that I so often get the maths wrong that I stick with the more tedious gridding approach.

The processes of enlarging drawings by grid scaling are the same whether you are working direct from a photo, from computer-produced 'charcoals', or from the not to scale plans books. First measure the total length of the bird (top of head to tip of tail) on the drawing/photo that you have. Let's say it is 4in (10cm). Now look it up in a field guide to birds that gives dimensions. Most books give sizes in inches – the book says that the bird I want is about 14in long (35cm). So we now have to turn the 4in book drawing into a 14in tracing outline – an enlargement of 3.5 times. The outline of the bird in the book must now be drawn onto paper which has a faint 1in square grid marked on it. These can be bought as flip chart pads at most graphics/art shops.

So 1in (2.5cm) of my original drawing will cover three and a half squares of the pad. This is a little too difficult to work with so I want to mark off my drawing with a grid such that one square of now gridded original will equate with one 1in (2.5cm) square on the pad. 4in (10cm) (the image's length in in/cm) is divided by 14in (35cm) (the bird's true length) and this shows that the grid should have squares of 0.2857 (rounded up to 0.286). My table of decimal equivalents shows that the squares should be about 19/64th inch (calculators may be used!).

Absolute decimal point accuracy is not necessary as most reference books give the bird size as being between two limits. My 14in (35cm) bird could be anywhere between 12in (30cm) and 15in (38cm).

Using a setsquare, lines are drawn along all four sides of the bird drawing and these are marked off every 19/64th of an inch. The marks are then joined to form a grid. Now looking at each square on the original you can see where the line you

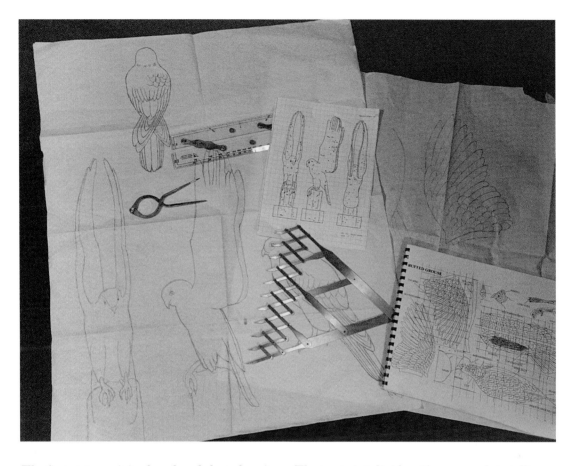

The first step – original and scaled-up drawings. The ten-point dividers (from a market stall) are very useful.

wish to copy enters and exits each square. This can then be re-created on the squared paper. Again perfect accuracy is not necessary and you will quickly see where a line needs final adjusting to make a clean curve or line.

There are some readily available tools which can speed up many stages of the process. A set of parallel rules certainly eases the drawing of the grid, and on a second-hand tool stall at a market I acquired a scaling tool that I can best describe as a 10-pointed set of dividers. Setting the first pair of points to the required 19/64th inch automatically fixes the correct spacing on the other nine.

Unfortunately, in most of the books that do not have full lifesize outlines each drawing is to a different scale, and certainly it is very difficult to get photos all to the same scale. Where there is uniformity in the scale of the illustrations you will be working with, you can make yourself a standard overlay grid by drawing lines on a transparent sheet using waterproof black ink. Clear transparent file covers from the stationers are ideal. Unfortunately, you normally have to end up gridding each new drawing individually.

Many artists now use projectors or simplified epidiascopes to produce outlines. Sometimes old epidiascopes can be picked up in junk shops very reasonably. Mine cost me £20 and then a further £25 to get all the mirrors re-silvered. In fact the better art shops sell neat little print projectors at somewhere between £100–300 each. With these, photo prints or sketches can be projected direct onto a drawing-board and can be scaled up or down to produce exactly the size of image required. Sitting to one side so as not to get into the beam you can quickly trace the outline of the projected image.

All you need are large sheets of white paper (usually 'Cartridge Paper' or a flip chart pad); some soft pencils – 2B drawing pencils being ideal; and a generously used soft eraser.

With the working size profile drawn out you can now sketch in the detail and here you will need to turn back to your bird-watching reference books. Most of these have only tiny illustrations – fine for bird spotting, but not very good for providing painting detail. You will have to search for books with large illustrations – often colour sketches. Some of these appear regularly on bargain book-stalls and can be very useful, and there are now the excellent bird and nature magazines with an abundant supply of good pictures.

A few of the more serious bird books have detailed drawings of the general anatomy of birds. It is useful to have a sketch of the skeleton, but it is essential to have annotated drawings of the main feather patterns. Most carving books refer to the various feather groups by name and in conversation with other carvers you will find that they also all use the proper names. The following drawings are there-fore important – it is useful to have a photocopier blow-up of the drawing pinned up on your workshop wall.

Of course the specific feather shapes and arrangements differ from bird to bird, but all have the same basic and clearly defined groupings.

On your drawings you should now carefully mark in the position of the eyes and outline all the main feather patterns using the exact arrangement and shapes that apply to your bird. It is at this point that most books fall short, and in the end you may still have to go to a natural history museum and make your own feather arrangement sketches.

By now you will be building the collection of feathers we mentioned a few moments ago. Unless you intend to only ever make wood carved and slick types of bird, I believe that a feather collection becomes essential. The study of the barb

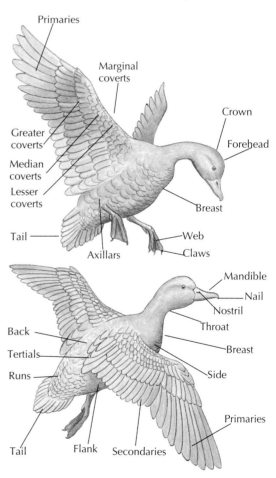

Main features on a duck – the feather groups.

orientation and profiles of the feathers on different parts of the bird will certainly help you to achieve realism. If you have a fly fishing friend who ties their own flies they will be able to supply you with a small collection of all the different feathers that you need.

Most experienced carvers also have a small collection of stuffed birds. Licensed taxidermists will take birds that have been accidentally or legitimately killed and stuff these. To ensure that no protected species is deliberately killed, the birds are registered with the DOE (Department of the Environment) and will have a little registration ticket attached to the foot. My collection includes a Buzzard, a Barn Owl, a Pintail, and a pair of Teal. The Barn Owl and the Pintail I have reproduced several times. All were bought from a South Coast taxidermist named, believe it or not, Kenny Everett! Soon after buying them I found that the previous owner of the Pintail had been Judith Nicoll.

The real value of a stuffed bird is not the provision of a specific model to copy, but is the permanent source of reference on feather layouts.

Some people may not like the next suggestion, but it does make a lot of sense. Buy a freshly shot duck and take pictures of it. Photograph all the details from two or three points of view. Take pictures of the feet, the head, the beak (particularly the underside), and the feather layout on the back. The most important of all is to stretch out the wings and then take a series of pictures of the wings as you fold them back in. The first thing that you will find that will surprise you is that the outer section of the wing folds in and tucks under the inner section. In the technical jargon of our drawing opposite, the Primaries and Greater coverts fold in under the Secondaries, Tertiaries and Median coverts.

You may be interested in one other source of reference. There are, around the country, a small handful of suppliers who service the needs of decoy carvers. From some of these you can buy study pieces. There is a range of castings taken from the work of some of the world's greatest carvers, there are also study bills in resin which have been taken from different species of real birds. Two suppliers now carry stocks of sets of excellent plans for a wide range of birds.

Your work in tracing outlines, sketching in feather patterns, and the inadequacy you have found with most reference books may have led you into your final stage of development.

One or two stuffed birds provide essential reference. Each has a DOE ticket with the license number, showing that the bird was not illegally killed. The birds with raised wings provide many carving problems!

Left: *Green-Winged Teal diving. This is an artificial pose created by the taxidermist. Note the very fine vermiculations (the multiple lines on some feathers).*

Bottom: *The wing half-folded, the outer section is beginning to tuck in under the inner wing.*

Right: *The underside of the wing. The primary and secondary feathers are very evident. The fold joint can be seen in the middle of the trailing edge.*

Below: *The wing extended as in flight.*

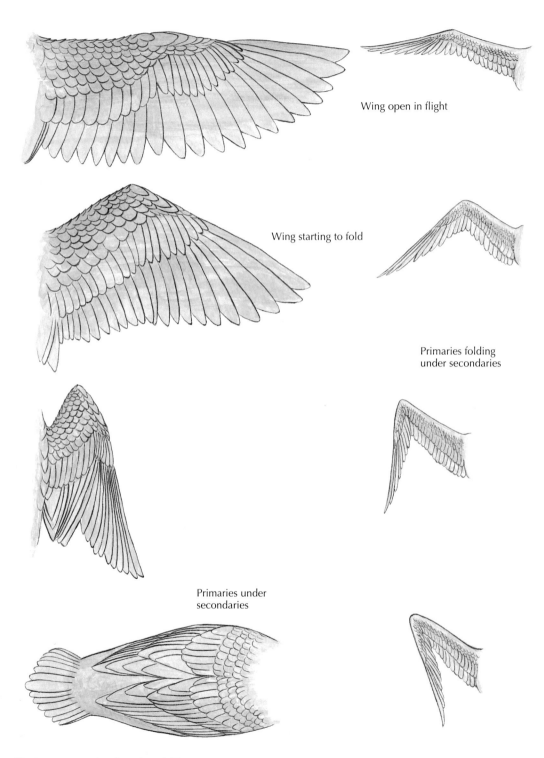

Wing open in flight

Wing starting to fold

Primaries folding
under secondaries

Primaries under
secondaries

Various stages in the wing folding process.

A substantial part of this chapter has been based upon the notion that you will quite quickly become dissatisfied with published plans – they no longer give you what you really want. So how about setting yourselves a long-term goal – that is, of being able to produce your own original carvings from drawings of birds in natural poses and displaying behaviour patterns that you have directly observed and sketched in the field. With the sketching of feather patterns that you have already done in museums and from stuffed birds you could be half way there.

Some carvers start with a highly developed perceptual ability. In their minds they can see and manipulate shapes in space. Some do not even need plans; they can take a block of wood, sketch on it a vague outline, and then carve out a beautiful accurate shape. They can probably draw well too. They are the sort of people that are referred to as 'born' artists or born sculptors. I am sorry but artists are not *born* – they are trained (or self-taught). They spend or have spent time learning their business just as you are doing with your bird carving. The main difference between the artist and the person who 'can't draw a thing', is that the former wants to draw (or paint) and is prepared to devote the time to developing the necessary skills; and that the other doesn't, so hasn't bothered! And you do not need to go to art school.

If you really think that you can not draw, there is one book that will put you right. It is not the easiest of books to read, but four of my friends who 'couldn't draw' have become part-time artists who now regularly sell their sketches. The book is *Drawing on the Right Side of the Brain* by Dorothy Edwards. It is on the shelves of most public libraries, but as it takes about a couple of months to work through you will probably want your own copy. 'Yes!' you are saying, 'but I don't want to draw pictures of birds, I just want to produce carving plans.' I contend that in the end the two can not be separated, and that whatever your starting point, they will eventually merge. But let's not talk any more philosophy – like the Edwards' book we will focus upon practical details.

The book says two things that will be important to us. First, that in nature there is no such thing as a line – there is simply a boundary between two planes. There is not a line around the 'profile' of a duck swimming on a pond, there is merely the boundary between the brown feathers of the bird and the greeny olive of the surrounding water. The significance of this will become more apparent later. The second thing that the book encourages is that in sketching that boundary do not try to draw a duck, but merely trace out curves, angles and distances. Draw what you see, not what you think you are looking at. Interestingly this is exactly what you were doing a few moments ago when tracing the entry and exit points and the adjoining lines as you transferred the information from one box on your gridded picture to the full-sized box on the plan drawing. The fact that you were trying to reproduce the outline of a bird is actual a total irrelevance while you focus upon getting each individual square right. What you have to put down on paper are lines of a required length, angle, radius and so on, that when seen as a whole, look like what we know as a duck.

Sketching in the field you can use your pencil held at arm's length and scale off the size with your thumb. Start by measuring a key feature then scale everything against that. Let's say you started with the length of the bill. Now every other part of the bird has to be seen as so many bill lengths. By tilting the pencil you can get the angle that the feature is above or below your datum. The principle is the same whether in the field or the workshop.

Obviously you will not start by making good sketches in the field, unless you already have drawing talents developed elsewhere. You will be starting with the scaling up of photos and other drawings. It is almost drawing by numbers. Do enough of this and eventually you will find that you now no longer need the assistance of an overlaid grid. Now you really are only one small step away from being able to make satisfactory field sketches.

Many of you will not be convinced. We develop mind-sets. 'I can't draw!' you tell yourself – and then you (subconsciously) make sure that you prove it. In Dorothy Edwards's book, and this will be the last time it is mentioned, there are sketches done by adults that look like the sort of stick people drawings often done by children at play group. These were drawn by people (students and adults) entering her programme. There are then drawings that the same people did three months later that many artists would be proud of.

Even if you are still at the gridded drawing stage, get yourself a little pocket drawing book, some 2B pencils and an eraser and take it with you. When you have a few minutes to spare, wherever you are, sketch something. Incidentally, don't wait until you find a bird to draw, start with buildings, parked cars, station benches – anything that catches your interest. However, when you do see birds, particularly birds in flight, sketch them. Try to get two or three pencil strokes which give the essence of the line of a bird in flight. You are not looking for detail now, but just quick impressions of posture.

There could come a day when you will get just as much satisfaction from sketching birds in the wild as you ever did from carving them in your workshop.

Well, by a circuitous route, and through many diversions, we have reached the stage when we have a three-plane plan of the bird we now want to carve. It is either in a plans book, or sitting on your own drawing-board. You now need a sheet of tracing paper, sheets of carbon paper and a pencil. Make a tracing of each of the three views and then retrace these directly onto the top and side of the block you will be working with. The front view is used to cut a plywood sizing template for the cross-section.

— 3 —

IT IS JUST A PIECE OF WOOD

Some people come into carving with little or no knowledge of the different types of wood available or of the properties of the various species. They quickly find that they need some understanding of the nature of the material that they will be working with. Of course there will also be those who start to carve birds having had some previous involvement in another area of woodworking and who already broadly understand timbers but who now need to know which woods are best for carving and why.

As identified earlier, there are a number of different styles of carving; each has a more appropriate range of woods to work with. To an extent, once you have chosen the style, you have, as it were, chosen the wood. If we look at some of the basic properties of wood we will see why this is so.

Wood can be crudely described as a vegetative material that consists of bunches of cellulose fibers or tubes that are bonded together in a woody matrix and that run up and down the tree. It is the lie of these fibres that gives what we commonly call 'grain'. So the grain of the tree always lies up and down the trunk or along the length of the branch. The tubes carry sap – the life-blood of a growing tree. Through a process of photosynthesis that occurs at the leaves the sap is turned into cell-building material that then develops as a mantle over the existing wood of the tree. Each year the cells actually form as a layer of new growth over the whole tree so trees grow fatter and taller because a new layer has built up over

the old. In broad terms the wood that develops 1mm or 1 metre, or 50 metres above the ground always remains at about that height.

During the early summer the new growth accelerates and is very thirsty; it requires more and more sugary sap to turn into new growth cells. It is also very vulnerable and would quickly dry out if exposed to the hot sun. It therefore has an inert protective sun shield/raincoat – the bark.

The arteries or tubes that carry the sap to the growing area are large. In the different tree species the actual diameter of the arteries varies in size and again, in broad terms, the softer the wood the bigger the tubes – and vice versa. In the spring and summer months when the photosynthesis process is at its peak and the sap is really pumping around, the tubes bulge, and more and more new tubes develop. If you cut into them, the tree will 'bleed', often profusely. Some saps are tapped for use – birch sap for making wine, maple sap for maple syrup, even our cars ride on tree sap – the rubber of our tyres. If you take too much sap or remove the bark so that it dries out, the tree will die.

In the autumn and winter months there is little or no sap movement and the outer layers of tubes dry out and collapse. The annular rings in the trunk show the lighter coloured thick bands of summer tubes followed by a thin darker band of the winter tubes that have collapsed.

If you look at a cross-section of the tree, you can see the thicker bands or rings of

*How many birds in these trees? –
Thousands! An avenue of mature
Lime trees at Sudeley Castle
(Gloucestershire). Lime is the
most popular carving wood.*

growth in wet warm summers, and the thinner light-coloured rings of long dry summers each separated by the thin dark bands of winter's slumber. Each summer the prevailing climate of the year leaves its own distinctive fingerprint within the tree and recognition of this has led to our ability to date pieces of wood that are centuries old. The science of doing this – dendrochronology – is fascinating.

The life-cycle of the sap itself starts as moisture drawn up from the ground. Trees that have very large tubes (and therefore very soft woods) require a lot of moisture and therefore flourish on wet and boggy ground – for example, Willow and Alder. Trees with a much smaller moisture requirement grow more slowly and produce hard dense woods – for example, Arizona Mesquite and Mediterranean Olive. In tropical rain forests other factors prevail to produce fast-growing but dense-textured hard-woods.

The moisture from the ground contains dissolved minerals – it is some of these minerals that are converted to the sugars and starches that are part of the growing process. Some other minerals are not used in growth and some of these precipitate out inside the tree and build up in the sap

tubes – a process equivalent of a slow furring of the arteries! According to the tree species and the particular minerals it selectively draws in, these deposits develop a colour and it is this that gives the species-distinctive hues to the heartwood of many trees.

While the sap is racing through the fat outer tubes you do not get this mineral-deposit furring of the arteries and the outer layers of the tree remain 'colourless' – usually and almost universally a creamy white. A section through an African Blackwood tree will have possibly a 10mm wide white outer ring that then switches to black for the remainder of the thickness of the trunk.

As the inner tubes become increasingly redundant (and mineral-furred) the fibre walls shrink inwards. Hence after the first few years of growth the tree still expands outwards but there is a continued contraction internally. Obviously this means that the timber of the inside of the tree is becoming continually more dense.

In time the tubes in the very centre of the trunk – the pith – become totally redundant. They die off completely and begin to rot. The hollow tree has started to develop. Splits occur and rain carrying fungal bacteria percolates in, thus

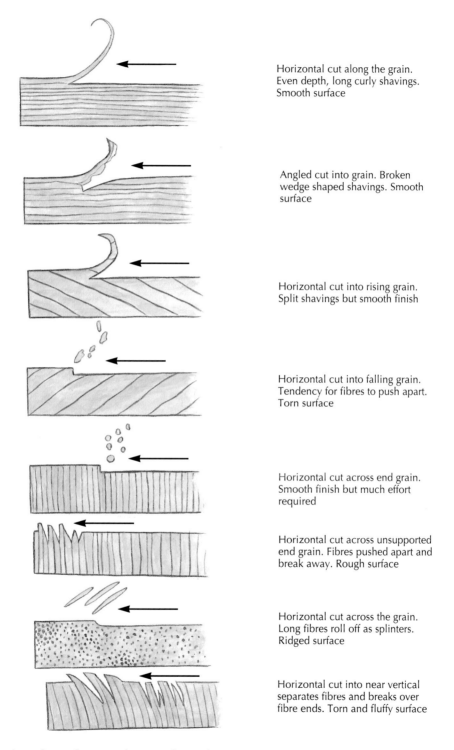

Horizontal cut along the grain. Even depth, long curly shavings. Smooth surface

Angled cut into grain. Broken wedge shaped shavings. Smooth surface

Horizontal cut into rising grain. Split shavings but smooth finish

Horizontal cut into falling grain. Tendency for fibres to push apart. Torn surface

Horizontal cut across end grain. Smooth finish but much effort required

Horizontal cut across unsupported end grain. Fibres pushed apart and break away. Rough surface

Horizontal cut across the grain. Long fibres roll off as splinters. Ridged surface

Horizontal cut into near vertical separates fibres and breaks over fibre ends. Torn and fluffy surface

Cutting along, down and across the grain.

Cutting across the grain can lift off 'splinters' – bunches of fibres.

accelerating the decay. It does no harm to the health of the tree and life continues to push outwards and upwards.

In a few moments we will look at one of the worst problems that this growth pattern can cause us carvers – splitting or checking in the wood.

Before considering the specific implications to the carver, there are yet one or two other basic mechanical/physical aspects to recognize.

The bigger the natural size of the diameter of the tree's tubes, the longer the fibre cases tend to be. It is often the softest of the timbers that have the longest and most clearly defined fibres. One of our favourite carving woods is, however, an exception to this.

Think now of a fibre being like a bamboo cane. In the centre is the hollow tube, around which is the fibrous casing or wall of the tube. In fact the wood of the bamboo is itself thousands of tubes all bonded together, but for the moment think of the cane as being a single fibre. Try to break the cane across its width and you will find it extremely difficult. To start with it will bend and when it finally gives the break will be jagged often with long splinters up and down the length. Try to

cut across with a knife and it is almost impossible. Now cut down the length from either end and the cane will readily split into two half-width canes. In splitting it down with a knife you have actually been parting the fibres that make up the cane's walls.

The bond that binds together the fibres of the cane, and indeed of any piece of timber, is much easier to break apart (or cut) than are the actual walls of the fibres themselves. The mechanical strength (resistance to shearing or breaking) is much greater across the fibres or grain than it is along them.

When we cut along the grain we are really separating adjacent fibres by cutting along the bonding material. When we cut across the end of the block of wood (or saw through the block) we are cutting across the middle of the fibres themselves, and the wood is much more difficult to cut in this direction. Now if we cut across the surface of the block at right angles to the grain our cutting tool edge will seek the easiest passage, through the bonding rather than through the walls of the fibres. What tends to happen is that fibres are pushed from their bonding and come away as splinters. Here the tool's edge is separating the fibres by breaking the bonding along their length.

Most tree species tend to true vertical growth with new even layers being formed each year. In forests the canopy seeks the sun to maximize photosynthesis. Hence adjacent trees vie with each other to be the tallest and get the most sun. The result is that the arteries shoot straight upwards.

Not all timber has a clean grain running straight from one end to the other. For a whole variety of reasons the growth pattern might be modified. Wet and dry seasons make a difference. Prevailing winds can give trees permanent bends. Open positions can cause flexing and the development of internal 'stress' lines. Freak seasons, differential shading from the sun and other factors can give areas of stunted new growth. A burr canker growth on the side can push its 'roots' into the trunk and disturb the vertical tubes. Or simply a branch may push out, or the trunk may fork. Any one of these can cause a distortion in the straight-through grain pattern. In the days of galleon building many angled timbers (knees) were required. These were cut from trees where there was a branch going off at an angle to the trunk and these were then trimmed to ensure that there was a true grain running from end to end of the knee.

Our next concern with the wood we use is what happens to the timber once it is cut from the tree – and the importance of the time of the year that the tree was felled and cut up.

The sap flow starts vigorously in the spring, peaks in early summer and then begins to fall back. In the depth of winter there is little movement of sap and the tree ceases to take up moisture from the ground. If you fell a tree in early summer,

sap will pour out of the cut – the moisture content of the timber will be at its highest. Dependent upon species (the bigger or smaller its fibres and arteries) the natural moisture content in a standing tree could be 80 per cent or more. If you fell the tree during the winter months – wet as they may be – the moisture content of the wood will be at its lowest level. The moisture is in two forms. First is the free moisture – the moisture within the 'tubes'. The second form is moisture locked within the fibres of the tubes.

If you fell a tree in early summer, the locked-in moisture will be about 35 per cent and the free water at maximum. If you fell the same tree in the period from November to February, the fibre saturation level will be about the same, but the free water level could have dropped 20–30 per cent – that is, the overall moisture content may have dropped as low as 60 per cent. But remember that these figures are species specific.

If you cut the felled tree into rings (a thing you should never do except for

Less dense woods with broad annular rings

Shrinkage greatest in large, sap-filled outer rings

Contracting tensions

Wood of outer ring not strong enough to resist tensions

10–20% Shrinkage around radius

2%–5% Shrinkage in diameter

Radial checks develop splitting down in to the heartwood. Large wide splits

More dense heartwood with small narrow annular rings

Shrinkage still greatest in outer rings but these are smaller and contract less

Pulling force caused by contracting outer rings

Splitting tension resisted by strength of wood

Shrinkage pulls on centre which pulls heartwood apart. Small splits occur in the heart

Shrinkage in wood as it dries.

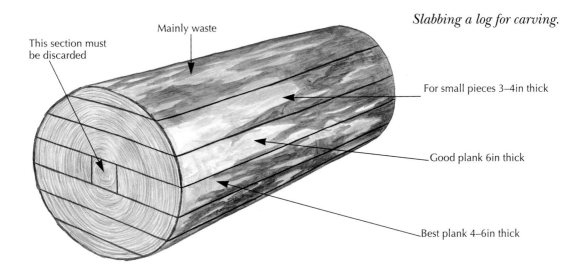

This section must
be discarded

Mainly waste

Slabbing a log for carving.

For small pieces 3–4in thick

Good plank 6in thick

Best plank 4–6in thick

firewood), even rings of 4 or 5ft (1.2 or 1.5m) in length they will start to dry out from the ends. The free moisture is the first to go, and as the arteries drain and the tubes start to contract, they shrink in girth and not in length. It is only later that the fibre saturation moisture level starts to fall.

The arteries nearer the heart of the tree have already contracted somewhat over the years so they have less to shrink than those towards the bark. In extreme cases you can get 10–18 per cent more shrinkage in outer rings than in the heartwood. Obviously the wood will then split. As the fibres shrinking at different rates tear themselves apart, you will get radial checks – wide at the outside where shrinkage is greatest, tapering to vanish just short of the centre.

In no time at all that wonderful piece of timber that you had stacked in your yard – that huge eagle that you were going to sculpt – is now only fit for the log basket. There are two things to do. First the log or trunk should be as long as possible – certainly of an unmanageable size! The bark must be left on and the ends of the log sealed and the whole protected from direct sunlight. Sealing the ends means liberally coating with wax. You can either

melt on paraffin wax, or give several coats of emulsified wax sealant. Then secondly the log must be cut up within a month or two into planks that are less likely to split. We have all shed bitter tears – many times – at the loss of logs we have kept too long, particularly if we paid carving not firewood prices for them.

To then further reduce the risk of splitting you have to slab or plank the wood so that each piece is composed only of similar parts of the tree – ie, it is either all softer outer timber or all denser inner wood. What is vital is to ensure that you do not have any piece which has the very centre of the trunk or branch running through it.

I have recently been offered a storm-felled lime tree. Most of it will be cut up for sale as fire logs. A chain mill will be brought on site and about a third of the trunk will be sawn into 5 and 6in (12 and 15cm)-thick planks. The centre plank will then be cut to remove a 6in (15cm) square baulk which will contain the heartwood of the tree. This too will be logged for firewood. The planks will then be cut into just-manageable 5ft (1.5m) lengths, and these will be carefully stored to air dry. There really is no other answer.

The planks will be stacked to allow controlled drying. This means three things: spacing them with small sticks to allow through passage of air between planks; a free passage of circulating air around the stack (not in the corner of the shed); and protection from direct sunlight. Even then it pays to end-seal the planks or slabs.

At this stage it is not likely to concern you greatly – it is of much greater interest to furniture makers and those using dimensional timbers – but during drying the planks will shrink only fractionally in length but by as much as 18 per cent in width and thickness. A plank with one edge in inner wood and one edge in outer wood will dry wedge-shaped in section.

If your finished work is likely to end up in a centrally heated room you must anticipate that its final environment will have a humidity level varying between 8 and 12 per cent. You must therefore anticipate that your piece of work will eventually reach this level.

As a carver of small songbirds you will only be using thinner slabs. But if you are making life-sized decoy ducks, you will probably need 5–6in (12–15cm)-thick planks.

In controlled air-drying you can expect most timbers to take one year for every inch of thickness to get down to the 15 per cent which is probably the desired working (and workshop) level. For planks over 4in (10cm) thick you double the drying time – hence a 6in (15cm) plank could take 12 years. It is suspected that some timbers over 6in (15cm) never dry – 10in (25cm)-thick oak beams removed after 400 years in a church roof were still green in the centre. Oak is usually given three plus years per inch of thickness to air-dry by the better timber-yards.

For thicker planks the kiln-drying processes of the average timber-yards are highly suspect. They tend to dry too quickly. This superdries the outer zones while leaving the core quite damp. Stated moisture content is often based upon a reading taken only about 1cm under the surface. Later, as the residual moisture capillaries out from the core towards the surface where it evaporates, the planks can split – long after they have been 'dried'.

Does it all matter? Again, it depends. The timbers mostly used for bird carving are fairly stable and unless extremely badly cut (the heartwood left in) they rarely split. If on the other hand you are producing carvings that will be left in polished wood finishes you will often use the more highly figured woods and some of these can be distinctly 'flaky' if not properly dried.

There is one area of work in which concern with drying and contraction is vital, and this is in laminated pieces. Clearly the two or more layers of the laminate must either not shrink at all, or must shrink equally and in the same direction. The idea of laminates that are plied (alternating long and cross-grain layers) is a short road to disaster.

Similar caution has to be exercised over carvings where you use inserts – you must use timbers with matching moisture contents, and this must be close to the expected ambient humidity of the position where your finished piece will reside. It is safest to expect the destination to be a centrally heated room where the heating is turned off in the summer – this will give an expected range of about 10–40 per cent humidity (and very much higher on some days). In carving birds with wings raised or in 'in flight' postures the grain usually runs down the body and then out towards the tip of the inserted wings. This means that at the point where the wing slots into the body you will have two pieces of wood with grain at right angles. Even with two pieces with matching moisture contents you will now have different degrees of shrinkage, and the glue joint will almost certainly give. We will see that one way of dealing with this is to use glues that flex and to make feather inserts to mask the joint (*see* Chapter 7).

Let's now look at the bird carver's concerns regarding grain. In fact there are three issues. First, in polished natural wood carvings our concern is to orientate the bird to feature the best aspects of the grain or figure. With some woods with a strong parallel line figure a simple horizontal fore and aft grain is most attractive. Sometimes if the fore and aft is placed on edge the two side pouches of the wings will appear as a series of concentric circles – again very effective. There may be differential patches of colour and we may be able to develop a carving with contrasting head and body. Occasionally we have happy accidents where, as the carving develops, a particular and unexpected feature of the figure begins to stand out. Equally we sometimes reveal hidden knots and flaws.

Unfortunately, we can not allow our desire for dramatic figure or visual impact to totally override our mechanical common sense. We have to orientate our bird within the timber in such a way that the carving will be structurally sound and will not snap at critical points. You can not carve a wader with its long neck and spindle legs from a single piece. You would not even get it from the workshop to the shelf above the fireplace before the legs had broken! The legs of realistic carved waders and others are usually made of wire and plastic wood, or are bought ready made in cast pewter.

Let's look at my favourite bird (a love shared with many carvers, twitchers and collectors) the Curlew, as this best illustrates most of the mechanical problems.

First, the curved beak. Carved with the body from a single block this would be extremely weak and would be broken within days (even if you managed to finish the bird). Even if carved from a separate inserted piece you could not get continuous grain down the length of the curved beak. To cope with this you first carve a straight beak along the length of true grain, and then steam or heat bend it to the required curve before gluing it into a 'jaw' hole. Obviously you do not have the

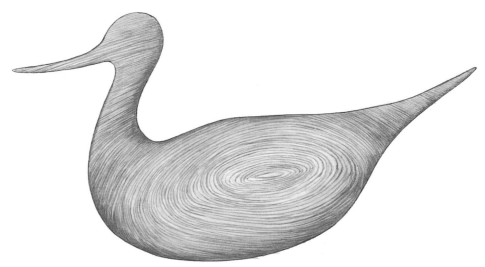

Making the most of the grain.

wingtips too cocked up. The legs have to be made up with at least a metal core or are simulated by mounting the bird on a length of dowel.

But what about the neck? If the grain runs true down the body, then the neck is obviously going to be cut across the grain. You have a choice. You could cut a separate neck and head piece with the grain running up it and then insert this into a recess in the body, or you may decide to accept the risk of the weaker cross-grain neck. The choice will be determined by a number of factors. If the carving is for exposed polished and highly figured wood, you probably do not want a glue joint with an obvious break in the figuring. With a less dramatic figure and a less stark grain change you may accept a carefully fitted joint – even possibly to feature the change in grain. Here the neck would be recessed into or dowelled onto the body and the joint then faired off. If the carving is to be feather-burnt then you can often burn feathers across the joint and thus completely mask it. In this case, a flat face-to-face dowelled and glued joint will suffice. If the bird is to be painted then a separate neck will probably be used as this is timber efficient and any sort of joint will be painted over.

While we are primarily interested in hue and figure for polished wood birds, our main concerns with feather-burnt and decorated birds is carveability and only then, with mechanical strength. 'Carveability' does also enter into our thinking with birds in polished wood finishes and there are some woods on which it is extremely difficult to get a good finish. Very attractive pitch pine is extremely fibrous and resinous. The surface fluffs up when carving across the grain then clogs up burrs of all grades, and in seconds blankets over any abrasive paper with resin build up. Finally the resin becomes 'dirty' and the bird loses all its attraction.

What then makes a good carving wood for realistic birds? Obviously realism requires fine and accurate detail. This in turn requires that the wood is easy to carve in any and all planes, and that any incised detail will remain crisp. Distinctly fibrous woods will not do this. We need woods

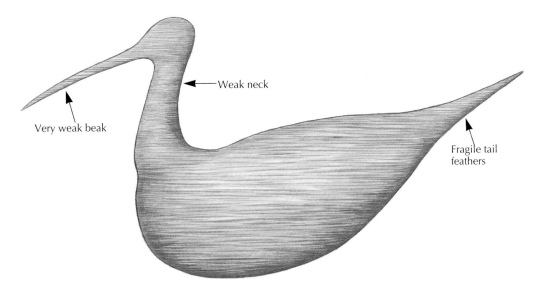

Weak points in single-block carving.

with no clearly defined grain structure. Certainly, good carving woods must be soft. However, while we want to be able to cut them easily we do not want them to be so soft that they bruise and will quickly develop marks of wear and tear. Easy cutting is that which can be done with sharp hand tools (knife, chisel and gouge) that do not need the impetus of a mallet!

There are two woods that best meet these criteria and there are then a number of also-rans. In America they use either native Basswood or imported Jelutong. The alternative US name for Bass is Linden. Linden is also the Dutch and German name for *Lime*! Basswood is actually a species of lime. In the UK we carve in either Lime or Jelutong – once again two nations separated by a common language.

Incidentally, very few textbooks make this cross-connection. The name Linden has vanished from common usage in England, yet once we wooed our maidens under the 'Linden Tree', the broad and abundant leaf making an ideal bower! Lime is beautifully soft (but still quite reasonable on bruise resistance), and it is noted for the fact that is difficult to split –

in any direction! It is often not easy to detect the lie of the grain and you can even cut into rising end grain without knowing that you are doing so, if your tools are sharp enough.

Jelutong is equally soft and bruise resistant, but it will split along the grain; it is therefore a little more fragile when you are cutting under the edges of feathers – breakout is not infrequent. It is more distinctly fibrous and grained than is Lime.

I obviously have a very clear favourite!

Amongst the also-rans are Poplar and Willow. Both are soft and easy to carve but both have long fibres, fluff excessively under burrs, and there is often breakout on fine detail. Both are very sensitive to bruising. One other wood that I have recently been experimenting with is Tulip and in the past Holly. Both are harder than Lime and therefore require more cutting effort. Chasing fine detail is not as easy but, once incised, lines hold particularly well. For me their breakout tendency is better than Jelutong. Both smooth and polish well and Tulip develops very nice coloration when well oiled.

— 4 —

MAKING THE BLANK

Let's start with the easy option! In a previous chapter mention was made of suppliers of casts of carved birds. That is not all they have to offer. Amongst the many other goodies they will have a list of pre-shaped blanks ready for carving. Many of these have been imported from the States and will be in Jelutong.

'Blanks' come in a number of different forms. With the crudest of all you get two squared blocks of wood, one of a suitable size for the head, and the other for the body of a named bird; these are sometimes called 'kits' and may include a pair of glass eyes and, only very occasionally, a set of drawings. Now you have to find and trace out the particular pattern of the bird that you wish to carve, saw the blocks into shape, and then carry on from there.

The first stage of refinement is again a two-part set but now the two pieces, head and body, are cut to profile. They are usually lifesize and fairly accurate in overall dimension. The corners on the top of the body will probably be angled off. Occasionally you will find that the body and head are both drilled for a fixing dowel, and it is likely that the eye sockets have been pre-drilled.

The beauty of the loose head is that you can mount it and set it to an angle of rotation so that the beak is not in line with the axis of the body. The straight fore-and-aft orientation, known as the 'standard pose', is a trifle boring!

In the next form of blank the head is already fixed on, or it may even be a one-piece carving. It is usually in a standard pose, but now all the shaping has been done for you. You can get straight on and start to carve in the feathers – or just smooth down the wood and apply paint. The species of wood will not be identified, but will almost certainly be Jelutong or Lime (or Bass).

There are a range of study birds available that are not of wood but of a compressed styrene or other composite material. Often these are moulded with all the feather detail 'carved' in. These can be used for painting practice without reducing their study value. Usually the carving detail is accurate, but is not quite as deep as I would like. With shallow carving it is very easy to clog up the detail by using paint that is a little too thick. We will be discussing painting later.

Actually a number of these detailed blanks have been moulded from an original which has been carved by one of the world's great decoy carvers. Such pieces are sold as 'Study Birds'.

So, you have a wide range of options. You can start with a cast feather-detailed bird ready for immediate painting; a shaped bird ready for smoothing and slick painting, or feather carving to whatever level you wish. Alternatively you can go to a profiled blank; or even a raw block of wood onto which you have to start by tracing a profile from a plan book; or you may really go back to basics, find your bird, study it, make your own plans and then cut it from a raw plank.

Wherever you start, it is almost inevitable that you will not stay there. Pre-shaped blanks in simple, swimming, head straight forward, standard poses may

Swooping House Martins by Judith Nicoll.

satisfy you for a while but there will come a time when you will want to take the next step. Feather-detailed realism will soon lead you into wanting to go for different poses and for birds set onto some form of mounting. It may be that the base is a simple piece of driftwood and you now carve your bird as it is coming in to land, on the branch. One day you will probably mount your hawk standing on its prey – fish, rabbit, mouse, or whatever. A pair of hummingbirds may have their beaks deep into carved flowers. Today it is rare indeed to see a single unmounted bird in any open exhibition or competition.

So let's take the first step starting right from the beginning – that of cutting our bird from the plank.

The chances are that you will want to carve more than one duck, and that you will not have finished the first before you start thinking about the next. Certainly your family or friends will be making encouraging noises and asking if you will make one for them also. Even if I thought that I was probably only ever going to make one carving of a bird of a particular species, I would still prefer to use two or three wooden templates to mark out the lines on the blank. Robust templates offer

Flying Swallows by Judith Nicoll.

several advantages. The first step is to trace the drawings that you have now developed or purchased onto a piece of thin ply. Greaseproof paper makes good tracing material. Using carbon paper, draw out onto the ply a full side and a plan view as a minimum. Trace both the outline and the main feather details. You may find that a front view, to give a third template, is also useful (but not essential).

Access to a sturdy band-saw is a godsend! It is one of the few pieces of heavy equipment that is almost essential to a bird carver. Unfortunately it does need to be of a fairly large size, as it is most frequently used on timber that is 4–5in (10–12.5cm) thick – hence a fairly large gape and a reasonable-sized motor is essential. I would strongly advise that you do not go for a Burgess or Black and Decker hobby-sized unit – these are very nice for small model-making but are not really tough enough for what we want. You will also need to take care over the choice of blades that you use. Often you have to cut around very tight radii. You can not do this with wide blades. Equally it is easier to follow a tight curve if the blade has widely spaced teeth.

Band-saw blades are classified by the number of teeth per inch of blade. It is known as the 'skip'. A good blank sawing blade is ⅜in (9mm) wide and 3 skip (three teeth to 1in (2.5cm)). Keeping the blade sharp helps considerably. Through your local supplier you should be able to find a saw sharpening service and the suppliers will sometimes send the blades away for you. Treated well, and occasionally re-sharpened, a pair of blades will last a long time.

Although you may use the band-saw, a fret or scroll saw is better for the accurate cutting of your templates; but these will certainly not cut blanks of the size you require. Obviously the front view will be an external template or a section of the body profile at the widest point and you will have to cut into the centre to make the shape. A large-sized scroll saw can not be justified if you are only interested in bird carving.

Ink over any feather and feature detail that you have traced onto the ply.

You will find that you use the templates for a number of tasks. Obviously their first purpose is to provide the outline on the block of carving wood. This is used to cut the blank to rough shape. Later, as you start to round off the bird, the templates are used to check the silhouette of the basic dimensions of the work as you progress. Finally, as you lay on and carve and/or paint the feathers a properly detailed template will provide a handy bench-side reference. This way you do not have to have your lovely collection of reference books or pictures constantly exposed to the dust of the workshop.

Perhaps the value of using plywood rather than card or hardboard templates will be coming clear. Obviously they last and can be used to make any number of repeats. They also provide a much firmer edge to guide the tracing pencil. For the few minutes that it takes you should trace in all the detail lines (feathers, beak and eye position). To make these marks permanent burn them in with your pyrograph tool. Oh! And while you are about it, burn the names of the duck or bird onto each template. It is a bit embarrassing to turn up at a show with an eider duck onto which you have inadvertently put an eagle's head! Yes! that is stupid, but I did once make a mongrel duck – the body and head were of different species.

It is very nice to start with a clean, squared blank of wood of exactly the right overall dimensions, and it does make the sawing out process much easier. It is, however, something of a luxury if you are going to carve a number of birds. At this stage you buy your timber by (the much cheaper) whole plank. I like to start with as large a plank as I can get. Some time ago I came across a small Devon timber-yard which had some 7ft long, 3ft wide, by 6in thick lime. It was not expensive and I brought back a trailer load. Of course, for a start you will probably buy single blocks of just the right size for the bird that you

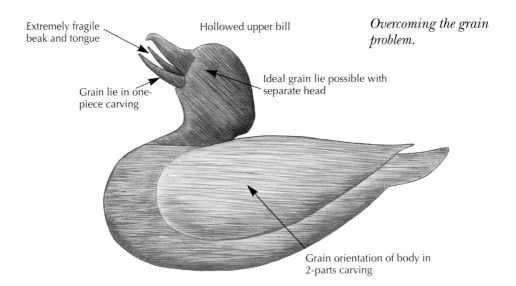

Extremely fragile beak and tongue

Hollowed upper bill

Overcoming the grain problem.

Grain lie in one-piece carving

Ideal grain lie possible with separate head

Grain orientation of body in 2-parts carving

are carving, but let's look to the day that you are buying at least moderate-sized planks.

To make the most of planks it is best to trace out a number of templates. Heads and necks can fit into the spaces over inverted backs. For reasons of both economy or design it is quite normal to cut the head and neck separately from the body. Detached heads can often be fashioned from offcuts. With everything carefully placed, waste can be reduced to a minimum.

You cannot however work to best-fit-to-the-plank criteria alone; each piece has to be oriented to give you a specific grain lie. With such a thing as the massive body piece mechanical strength is not so impor-tant; now your main consideration is getting the grain lie that gives you the easiest carving. Most of the body carving is along a fore and aft line so this is the ideal grain orientation. Hence the body block is traced along the plank. It normally does not matter whether it is the plan or the elevation template that is traced on the top of the plank. The thickness of the plank is now the only consideration.

Thin sections such as wingtips, tails,

necks and beaks can be very fragile – here the grain must run down the length of the component. Wing sections must always have grain from tip to root. If the bird is displaying with head back and beak inclined upwards, and/or the tail cocked, then head and tail will have to have grain on a different lie from that in the body. This will often mean that these elements of the carving have to be separate and be inserted into or spliced onto the body piece.

Again, as we identified when discussing woods, the position of the template will be adjusted to give the best figure in polished natural wood finished birds. Obviously you do still have to think about the mechanical strength of thin sections.

The careful placing of the templates on a large plank allowing only minimal spacing between each blank can easily give you an extra two or three birds; it can however also give you some problems. It may mean that you are having to band-saw a massive and unwieldy block of timber.

If you are aiming for economy, place the templates so that although there are overlaps there are one or two straight or diagonal lines across the block where it is

Two planks of Lime being marked out using templates. Plywood templates cost very little and can be used for repeats.

possible to use a chain-saw to render the slab down to more manageable pieces. A quite small electric chain-saw is very useful at this stage, but the chain must be kept sharp so that the saw can be kept to the cutting lines that you require.

In marking out by tracing around a wooden template with a carpenter's pencil you will naturally produce a drawing line that is slightly larger than the template. It is up to you whether you now saw inside, on, or outside the line. I like to work on or even just outside the line as this allows for any wander of the band-saw and provides a working margin for the later carving processes.

You can make the cutting-out process easy or difficult. Let's illustrate this by going back to the single nicely squared block approach and then consider what modifications we need to make when dealing with whole planks.

Position your plan template on the broadest face of the block and trace round it. Next position the side view template on the side of the block ensuring that the beak and tail tips correspond with the plan view markings (they will be the same distances in from the block ends). Trace this outline.

Now place the block flat on the band-saw table. I normally work with the elevation outline uppermost. Cut along the whole of the profile of the top of the bird. Try to make this one single pass right down one side from end to end. You may have to make small widening cuts to move around a particularly tight radius, but try to keep the overall cut continuous. Keep the main pieces of waste that you have cut away. Next, cut the other line of this profile – the underside of the bird. At the ends you may need to cut small wedges to notch the tail or to get in under the beak. Again aim for a single length main cut and keep the waste piece. You will end up with a good side profile of the bird – the positive – and two pieces of waste which will be the negative of the profile.

With three lengths of masking tape fit the waste back to the profile to re-form the original rectangular block. You can ignore any small wedges cut from the ends. There will be a tape wrap towards each end and one around the middle of the block.

Now replace the block on the saw table but this time with the plan view uppermost. By having reconstituted the block (with masking tape) it will have a firm squared base that again sits flat on the saw table. You now cut the whole top profile defining the sides of the bird, and because of the squareness of the taped-up block, sitting cleanly on the saw table, it is easy to cut the sides very accurately.

45

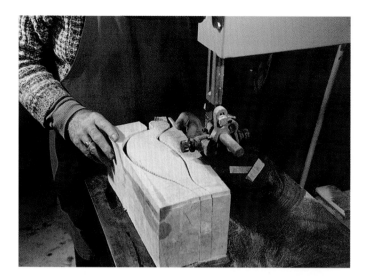

Cutting the blank from a squared block. The side view of the Curlew is cut with two long, continuous cuts; the waste is then taped back on.

The reconstituted block now has the top (plan) view traced on.

The block is cut from each end leaving a small uncut section in the middle. Finally the middle section is parted.

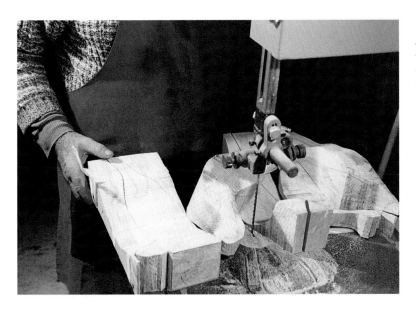

The blank emerges. Large pieces of waste are retained for heads and making thin section inserts.

An Owl and a Goldeneye are cut from a single block to reduce waste. The head on the template is then oriented to get the grain right for the beak and tongue.

You may find it easier to cut the plan-view lines with a series of four cuts. Cut in from either end but do not cut right through the centre wrap of masking tape. Only when all four cuts have been done do you cut through the final tape and join up to complete the cuts.

Obviously if you are sawing many blanks from a plank it is much more difficult. Here you will have only one view of the bird traced on the plank. Sometimes it will be possible to work broadly to the drawn lines and to reduce the plank into a number of near rectangular blocks. Often not! Certainly in cutting out the blanks try to leave one square edge, preferably the base.

The squared base will now sit on the table of the band-saw, but you will have to carefully trace the plan view onto the shaped top of the bird. Keeping the pencil vertical and ensuring that the eye is straight over the top will help. There will often be some freehand adjustment of the drawn profile before you start cutting.

The next step in cutting out the blank requires extreme caution and a firm grip.

The band-saw can be used to trim away

47

some of the corners of the blank to reduce the amount of subsequent rough carving. If you are going to try this you need to ensure that the bottom of the blank is resting firmly on the saw table and that the blank is well gripped at both ends. Use a pair of industrial gloves just in case of a slip. Take small cuts and make sure that the blank is angled so that there is a free way in and out for the blade. It is very easy to get it wrong and to go in too deep. It is also easy if the grip is not firm enough for the blank to rotate in the hands and to bind on the blade. The saw jams and the blade will kink. You will get a nasty shock and possibly a banged knuckle. The process requires bold determination – any lack of resolution and a lock up will occur. With a little practice however, you can remove quite a lot of waste and considerably reduce the crude carving.

You now have a one-piece, two- (separate head), three- (separate tail), four- or five- (wings) piece blank for the next process.

Some carvers using two- (or more) piece blank sets find it easier to do much of the shaping of the body before the head is attached. Certainly it can greatly facilitate the use of a draw-knife or spokeshave if the form is simple and uncluttered.

However, now is the time to make provision for fitting the head – even if it is to be actually glued on later. Place the head on the top of the body and mark off where you want it to sit. Sand the top of the body and the base of the head until you get a perfect tight abutment. Here a belt sander is very useful.

Next, mark off the dowel positions and drill the holes for 10mm dowels.

Cutting the blank is the most dangerous part of the decoy carver's tasks. It is well to always remember that woodworking machinery has the reputation of producing the highest number of accidents of any industrial sector. Most lifelong carpenters have one or more fingers missing. Often you have high-speed rotating cutters that, by the nature of the job you are doing, can not be fully enclosed or guarded. Spindle moulders and table routers are amongst the worst.

A tricky process. Taking the corners off on the band-saw. Done carefully!

Circular saws come high up the list. Band-saws too are not good. Power planer accidents are less frequent but can still be quite nasty – as the end of my little finger knows to its cost. In preparing blanks you must be particularly vigilant.

There is a real killer – it is dust. If all you ever do is chisel shape, gouge carve, and finish with scrapers you have little to worry about. However, few of us, even the most dedicated traditionalists, end there. Band-sawing creates a very penetrating and insidious dust. Arbortec and Kutzall power carving make masses of larger-particle dust. Etching and fine 'carving' with burrs mounted in Foredom, Dremmel or Minicraft tools make a nasty dust which is finer than that created by the band-saw. Sanding, particularly using power-driven discs, is probably the worst of all.

The dust from any wood is not good for you. Respiratory problems are common-place amongst long-term woodworkers. A few woods are lethal! The dust from some hardwoods can cause rashes – often to the wrists. There are also woods that are known to have carcinogenic dusts. Iroko makes nice polished wood carvings but its dust can be deadly.

Masks are not the most comfortable of things although some are a lot better than others. The small disposable face-masks are really not good enough. They are OK for a quick job where there is minimum dust and a very brief exposure, but anything beyond this and you need much better protection. Some of the close-fitting rubber nose and mouth enclosing face masks with disposable filter pads are very good, as are the helmet masks with a fan-driven filtered air supply. These latter are, however, quite expensive, but then so are replacement lungs! Actually, in terms of cost, the rubber face-masks with replaceable filters work out much cheaper (and are infinitely more effective) than packs of fabric masks bought in the local DIY store.

One little tip: if you do use a rubber mask it is as well to spray the inside with a disinfectant after each spell of use. It took me a long time to trace a recurring throat infection.

Finally on dust, and this is the most important of all; do not remove the mask once you have finished the dust-producing task. The worst dust there is is that fine stuff that hangs in the air for an hour or more after it has been created. The best advice of all is to find a mask that is comfortable, put it on as soon as you start any dust-making task and only take it off when you leave the workshop. I also try to make the band-sawing or sanding the last jobs that are done before leaving the workshop for the day – or at least for a major meal break.

The cutting tools that a carver uses should be as sharp as are many razors. Of course we are aware of that because of the hours we invest in sharpening them, so we do tend to be careful. But as you become involved in trying to achieve a particular effect it is all too easy to have a little slip. If, like me, you often carve onto your lap, wear a leather apron. A slip with a veiner can put a deep wound into the thigh. Never hold a piece in the palm of the hand and cut into it – in fact never have any one piece of your body in line with the direction you are carving.

THE CHIPS START TO FLY

Some people regard the next stage as the most enjoyable of the whole process. Here you take the sawn blank with all its angles and corners, and in a matter of an hour or so it is rounded and is beginning to look like a bird. It is the sheer enjoyment of this process that leads some of the more traditionalist carvers to use the same sort of hand tools that have been employed by woodworkers for generations. Each glide of the draw-knife takes you a step further down the road of shaping and smoothing and brings you nearer to the form that you require. The carving of wood with hand tools must be one of the most therapeutic activities devised by man. Other carvers, more interested in the finished results than in the carving processes, speed up the work by using the most aggressive of modern methods – Arbortec and coarse burrs, and the chips

fly in all directions. Everything is soon covered. What is that old adage about it being better to travel than to arrive?

You have enormous choice. If your sole purpose is to produce birds as quickly as possible, and you can justify the capital outlay, there are fully automated carving machines that will do it all for you. Here a computer-controlled router swings around over a table onto which the blank is clamped. You then need a gang of detail carvers and painters to cope with the output. One step down the line is the Dupli style carvers that will replicate virtually any carved form. Here you trace over the contours of a hand-crafted model or a finished bird with a stylus mounted on a pantograph. At the other end of the machine a ¼in router cuts away at the blank. With a careful choice of cutters, a very accurate, detailed representation can

The Duplicarver at work. These can produce amazingly accurate copies from a carved original.

be achieved. You are, however, still look-ing at a capital outlay of over £1,000 and you get none of the enormous satisfaction that you experience as you see the shape emerging under your own hands.

At the complete opposite end of the scale is a whittling knife (costing £2–3) which is kept sharp on the stone lintel of the cottage door.

Many carvers today use some form of power tool in the shaping process, so let's overview some of the most widely used devices starting at the upper end of the power scale. We will be looking more closely at the carving of detail in the next chapter.

LARGE CARVINGS

If you are making larger than life wood sculptures you may be attacking sections of tree trunk and will probably do most of your 'carving' with a chain-saw. Basic shaping is done with the length of the chain-saw blade and detail is then cut with the rounded nose. With a sharp chain a quite acceptable form can be achieved in ten or so minutes. At a recent agricultural show a forester was making swooping eagles in about that time. It is not as dangerous as it looks, but control of the cut is not easy and achieving exactly the result you require does take some practice. It is important that the saw is held firmly in both hands and that protective clothing is worn. Chain-saws can slip or kick back so the special padded trousers, Toe-tector boots, reinforced gloves and a hard hat with visor should be regarded as the minimum. Ear protectors are also widely used. Chain-saw carving is definitely not for the inexperienced nor the faint-hearted. It is also very messy and because of flying chips and fumes it is something that must be done out of doors. There are now one or two electrically driven

chain-saws that have sufficient power, but they are not the ordinary DIY jobs.

Obviously the chain-saw produces 'rustic' pieces and the sawn surface is often left as cut. It can be fun but the results are 'broad brush' to say the least of it!

Some carvers have developed skills in using the Arbortec for large sculptures. These are vicious but effective tools where a circular blade is fitted onto an angle grinder. The rim of the blade is profiled and sharpened to resemble the teeth of a chain-saw. In the early developments of this approach a length of chain-saw chain was actually used. This was held between two discs but was free to rotate inde-pendently of the retaining discs. As the head spun, centrifugal force caused the chain to drive. As a tool it was quite effective, but once any pressure was

A demonstration of chain-saw carving at Yandle's show. Full protective gear is essential.

51

A chain-sawn Eagle – quick, rugged and effective.

applied the chain stopped rotating. This made it much more gentle and controllable than the subsequent Arbortec.

For all its noise and power, the Arbortec is a wonderful tool – in the right hands and on the right job! It is cheap, and is ideal for working the harder, denser woods. Obviously, in addition to the cutter blade, you also need an angle grinder and some protective clothing. The plus side is that it removes waste very fast and, with practice, it can be reasonably accurate. The downside is that the process looks terrifying, and it creates a lot of small chippings which fly everywhere; the tool can also run away from you. Get the direction of approach or the angle of the blade wrong and in an instant it will bite into the wood, pull away from you (it can even be torn from your hands) and it will have put a nasty deep gash across your work. As a standard practice when cutting with an Arbortec I never lock the switch in the 'On' position but hold it down with my thumb. Now if the tool or my hands slip, the machine will come to a stop.

The best results are achieved by holding the tool firmly; one hand on the handle

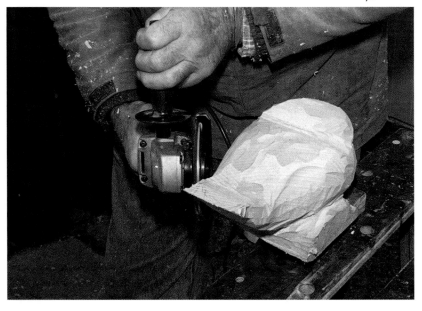

Fast rough shaping using an Arbortec blade on an angle grinder. A frightening practice and it is easy to overrun!

and one round the body with the thumb on the switch. Keep the blade in a near horizontal plane so that if it does kick it will sweep sideways. Now draw the tool towards you. This means that you are cutting with the side of the blade. Make any side-to-side cuts by starting on the right-hand side and work towards the left in a series of drawing-in sweeps. Keep the cuts shallow. Problems start when you try to take deep cuts, particularly along the line of the blade – the blade digs in, climbs up on its own circumference, and the tool jerks forward cutting the deep gashes.

When working on true to life-size bird carvings the Arbortec is a bit over the top even as a first stage shaper – except, possibly, on eagles, large owls, geese and swans.

The hand-tool-only approach to working on larger-than-life carvings is based upon the use of trimming axes and hand adzes. These require a lot of skill (as well as being kept very sharp). The difficulty is in ensuring that each blow is angled properly to cut away the timber but not to get buried in it or split off large pieces. Cutting along the grain is the most likely to cause splits, cutting across the grain takes forever. Most blows are therefore angled at between 30 and 45 degrees to the run of the grain. The greatest skill in using a carving adze is to get the sweep of the blade to follow an arc with the apex of the arc just cutting between 2 and 5mm into the wood and the end of the sweep bringing the blade back out of the surface.

With practice, skill can be acquired and the adze can be a very effective sculpting tool. The seats of some Windsor chairs and the tops of refectory tables are sometimes finished with adzes. This can give an even but slightly rippled surface. In the days before power planers a lot of country furniture was made this way. Here the adzes used were not the small hafted single-handers we use for sculpting, but were the long double-handers. Carvers

Hollowing out the underwing with a radius-face Spokeshave.

There is nothing like a traditional draw-knife for both rapid waste removal, and the fine planing of open expanses.

then stood on the seat or table top, feet apart, and swung the tool forward and back between their legs. It is said that some apprentice masters used to make their pupils take off their boots to ensure that they would be careful in the way they swung the razor-sharp tools. I prefer steel-capped boots!

For the next approach in this descending order of rough cutting speed we come back to the traditional methods of the decoyists. The best, again needing practised skills, must be the draw-knife, and this is certainly my own favourite. Here a sharp blade is held between two handles with which you pull the edge towards you. The blank needs firmly mounting and I find the best method is to wear a leather apron and to grip the blank between my thighs. In skilled hands the draw-knife is the fastest and most accurate method of shaping blanks.

The knife cuts very much like a chisel. It works best along the grain and on long straight cuts. Like a chisel it can also work well taking shorter shallower cuts across the grain. Much more power can be applied to it than to a spokeshave or chisel because you can use the full pulling power of both arms, and in this way it quickly outperforms the whittling knife and chisel. It can however, when pulled to the limit, exert a pull that is beyond the capacity of most ball-jointed carving heads, and at this level it demands a really strong pair of thighs. Fortunately such loading is not normally necessary – it only occurs when trying to take off a big corner working across the grain.

The draw-knife has one overriding advantage. It can be worked into shallow concave areas taking nice scooping cuts. As with a chisel the skill of draw-knifing is in the use of the bevel. In normal use the bevel is on top, hence the bottom of the blade sits flat on the timber. As the handles are drawn towards you the blade

is tipped about a degree and bites into the wood, you then control the depth of cut by the angle of the blade to the wood face. If you get it right you can draw off shavings similar to those produced by a hand plane. If the tool is sharp enough you can dig deeper and bring off chisel-sized waste. Go too deep and the blade stalls or draws off large, sheared splinters.

When working into a scoop the tool is inverted and it is the bevel face that is kept in contact with the face of the timber.

Going around curves does require more skill and an even sharper blade.

Many of us use draw-knives to shape most of the blank. To get a better, near final finish to the surface we then use another traditional tool – although in most cases it will be a modern version. A great deal of the final shaping and smoothing is done with a spokeshave. I tend to work with three. Two have flat soles and one of these is set to a coarse cut, the other for fine finishing. The third spokeshave has a radiused sole and is used for working concave areas, but I find that I can often cut a deeper scoop and work in more awkward corners with the draw-knife than with a spokeshave.

There is one critical difference between the working of the two tools. Only if the blade of the knife is razor sharp and you have ultimate skill levels can you cut into rising grain. You must normally turn the work piece around and cut 'downhill'. With a sharp spokeshave set very fine uphill cutting is sometimes possible (but only when you have to!).

Once the cut starts, the curl of swarf on top of the knife blade pushes the blade down and under the edge of the grain – this in turn will push the edge in even deeper and the cut can quickly stall. To avoid this, once the cut has started the sole of the blade must be kept flat on the timber. If it tips at all, then a deep splinter is torn out. The soleplate on a spokeshave prevents this digging in – hence the possibility of cutting into rising grain.

A note of caution: the more heavily grained the timber the more important it is that you get the angle of attack right. However, assessing the run of the grain in the types of wood we use is not always easy, until you actually start to cut into it with the draw-knife. It can be particularly difficult when working around a corner where the grain is diagonal. On one side of the corner it can be going one way and on the other side in the opposite direction.

Anybody can use spokeshaves and most people find the process very satisfying. Shapes emerge, nice curves develop, grain appears and the surface burnishes. Obviously the blades need to be kept sharp and should be set so that they can only just be felt below the soleplate. If the depth of cut is kept fine, the tool will work for some time before needing resharpening, and because of the ease of use they can be operated quickly and fast waste removal will result. As with the draw-knife the ideal normal plane of operation is along the grain on flattish surfaces, but they are quite at home tracing around convex curves. Cutting across the grain is possible but is greatly facilitated if the tool is held skew so that the edge is at 45 degrees to the run of the grain. Spokeshaves with a rounded soleplate will smooth into shallow concave surfaces, but this is not easy and is best limited.

Of course they are totally safe. The only injury that you can inflict with a spokeshave is if the blade catches and the tool rotates in your hands. When this happens the handle can bend back your fingernails – as an occasional guitar player I find my right-hand nails quite vulnerable! Using an industrial glove does help.

At this point a small diversion might be appropriate. Mention was made a moment ago of a Carving Head, and my own preference for gripping the workpiece between leather-clad thighs.

There are two forms of mounting devices used by carvers. One is the classic Carver's Screw. This is a long threaded device, which is pointed at one end for screwing into the base of the wooden block that is to be carved. The rod is passed through a hole in the work-bench and a butterfly nut then clamps the block to the bench.

For a bird carver these screws are not very useful. With the piece close to the bench there is not room to swing draw-knives or spokeshaves, nor to carve the undertail area with gouges. The use of spacers – pierced blocks of various thickness – can help.

The full set. Two traditional draw-knives; a modern Flexcut knife (surprisingly good); and a radiused and two flat spokeshaves.

Of greater utility are the ball-jointed carving heads which hold the piece a few inches up from the bench, and with the articulation of the ball joint allow the carving to be swung around for easier access to all zones. The disadvantage is that the ball clamp on some models will not hold against the pull on a draw-knife when you are doing the early, really rough work.

Both the fixed and the ball heads require a substantial hole to be drilled into the bottom of the carving. One make requires a hole of almost an inch (2.5cm) in diameter because it involves the use of threaded bushes. I prefer not to have filled holes in the bases!

There are two more power-carving approaches to look at while we are still at the rough shaping stage. These methods have been left to the end of this review as both directly overlap with two of the three principal methods used for working detail into the carving, and detail incision will be the main subject of the next chapter.

The first uses power-carving devices that are fundamentally motorized chisels. All use an electric motor to provide hammer blows to the end of a chisel or gouge blade. In America decoy carvers have had, for some time, access to a range of small units many of which were made in Japan. These, typically, had a fractional horse power motor with a right-angle geared drive at the end. The outboard end of the drive is fitted with a cam which rotates at high speed. Into the mouth of the tool you clip small cutters which are available in a range of sizes and profiles. Usually the blades are straight and have chisel, gouge or veiner profiles. In more recent years Bosch have introduced a tool of this nature into the UK market. They are sometimes called Power Chisels.

While lightweight tools of this type are useful for carving detail they are limited in their waste removal capability. The small blades blunt quite quickly, and if you try to

A carver's screw, and an articulated carving head for holding the workpiece to the bench.

take too deep a cut, the drive will stall. Unfortunately the blades produced for the Bosch tool are not satisfactory. The steel is too 'soft' and I find that the edges burr and micro-chip even when used on soft lime. I have tried to contact the manu-facturers to discuss this problem, but have had absolutely no response. The main problem with most small power carvers however, is that they are designed for only intermittent use and in long periods of rough carving the motors soon overheat.

Some time ago, Bourdet, a French company specializing in stone-carving tools, produced an outfit with a much bigger motor, a really heavy-duty flexible drive, and a hand-held drive head which will take full-sized carving tool blades. The hand unit is particularly nice. It fits well into the palm and only applies hammer blows when the blade is loaded – that is, when it is pushed against the wood.

The company does also produce a full range of blades with all the conventional carving blade profiles in absolutely superb steel. One of the Bourdet drivers is particularly robust and will stand a full day's continuous work, even on stone carving. The blades have a round tang, but bought in the UK they are a little expensive. However, unhandled blades

The Bourdet carving set.

A portable work table used for demonstrations (and in the garden working). Here it is set up with a Foredom carver.

can be bought direct from the well-known toolmakers Ashley Isles. These, their standard carving tools, normally have a tapered square section tang, but these can be rounded to size on a standard grindstone wheel. The Isles blades are wonderful. They are quite easy to grind to fit, the range covers every shape, profile and size of carving tool, they take a very keen edge and hold the edge for a considerable working period – and they are significantly cheaper than the French equivalents.

Obviously by using the larger patterns of chisel and gouge and with the power of the heavy-duty unit, you have an ideal combination for the rapid removal of waste, and for detail carving. They are very easy to work with and will enable you to carry on carving long after mallet-battered osteoarthritic hands will no longer allow

you to use a chisel and gouge (and it eventually comes to most of us!). My Bourdet gets more and more use day by day. The outfit is however a little expensive for the occasional bird carver, and is best thought of as a production tool (or a geriatric crutch!).

The second power approach is more likely to appeal as it is more versatile and is somewhat cheaper – although it does make a lot more mess. Here the rotary output of an electric motor is used to turn a burr or milling cutter. There are many sizes of motor used and a very wide range of cutters available. It is possible to mount cutters directly into the end of a die grinder, but these very powerful units

57

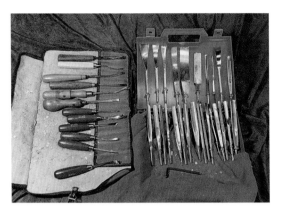

On the left my original carving toolset. On the right the blades for the Bourdet including those fashioned from Ashley Isles unhandled blades.

tend to be too fast (a single speed of upwards of 15,000RPM) and are heavy to hold. They are therefore difficult to control accurately. Of more use to the bird carver are two subsets of tools.

The first, and most widely favoured, uses a motor of up to a quarter of a horsepower driving a rotary cutter head through a flexible drive shaft. They are normally used with a foot-operated speed controller. Probably the two most popular makes are the Foredom and the Pfingest.

The second set are the smaller hand-held tools such as those from the Dremmel or the Minicraft range. The Dremmel runs directly off the mains while the Minicraft has a transformer with speed controller. Obviously these lighter units are not quite so appropriate when it comes to heavy waste removal – they are however much more friendly when incising fine detail, so we will come back to these again in the next chapter.

The range of cutters for all rotary tools is enormous, and can be divided into four categories.

The most aggressive, and certainly the ones used for waste removal and rough shaping, have nodules of tungsten carbide sintered onto a carrying mount. They are normally available in two shaft sizes – ¼in and ⅛in diameter, and three 'grit' sizes. There are then a number of profiles – cylinder, dome, bulb and pointed. For rough cutting the coarsest grit is used and with a ¼in shaft bit this means carbide particles of between 1 and 2mm. The ⅛in shaft coarse head burrs have carbide grains of about 0.5mm. A widely used variety come under the trade name Kutzalls. They are very efficient even on bulk waste removal, but they do produce huge quantities of medium and fine dusts. Incidentally Kutzalls are appropriately named – they are extremely good at removing skin!

The second category are the milling cutters. These may be made of high-speed steel or solid tungsten carbide – and the latter is greatly to be preferred for their long wearing ability. Again there is a huge range of available profiles and a wider range of drive shaft diameters. They work well, are very controllable, do not tear flesh if you slip, but even at high drive speeds they cut much more slowly than the sintered carbide heads. My set does not get very much use on roughing.

The next type of cutter is really used for detail work. They are normally available only in the smaller shaft sizes (⅛in and similar) – but still offer a full range of profiles. Again they are grinders rather than cutters, with grit sintered into a carrying head. Here, however, the grit is fine powdered diamond or ruby.

The grit stones often supplied with Dremmel and other kits are our fourth category. Their use in bird carving is fairly minimal being limited to smoothing or fine texturing.

Tungsten carbide burrs and cutters have two enormous advantages. The first, already mentioned, is that of extremely long-wearing durability. The second is that when clogged they can be cleaned very easily. Some timbers clog up cutters in seconds. Resinous pines are the worst, and

*Power-carving bits and pieces.
Kutzall and other burrs –
coarse and medium 'grits'.*

*Milling cutters in steel and
solid tungsten carbide.*

here the cutters need cleaning every few minutes. If, immediately it clogs, it is dipped in genuine turpentine and then wire brushed it can be cleaned quite quickly. Once the resin has hardened, then there is only one answer. You will not like the sound of this and will be nervous about trying it at first, but it works extremely well, and does not damage the cutter in any way. Just use a blow-torch and burn away whatever is clogging the heads! (Holding them with mole grips in the flame of the gas cooker works equally well.) In fact burning is the only way of cleaning a baked resin clogged cutter. I understand that the same approach can be used with ruby and diamond burrs but with these I rely on turpentine and a wire brush – and I *never* put them away dirty!

The greatest advantage of the rotary burrs is their total versatility. They can work along the surface – flat, concave or convex – or they can be pushed into the wood to bore holes. They can be driven

59

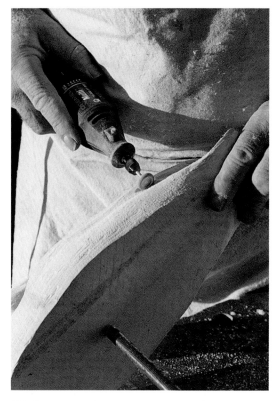

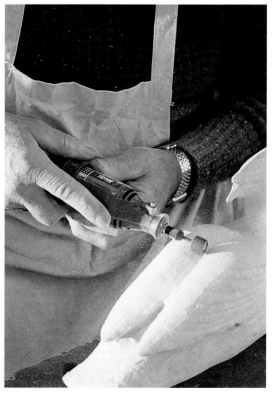

Undercutting the wings with a medium Kutzall in a Dremel Multi. The blank has a carver's screw inserted.

Smoothing hollowed areas with a small sanding drum.

hard for quick removal of mass waste, or very lightly to achieve quite delicate shapes. They work equally efficiently along or across the grain, even over end grain.

Obviously grinding does not remove waste as fast as does a draw-knife (or heavy powered gouge) but it does beat a spoke-shave – and you do have complete versatility in directions of attack. The greatest advantage is that you can get into any corner or hidden crevice. The coarse cutters do tear the surface of the wood and leave it very ragged, so you may need to go through three grit grades to get a working face for the detailed carving stage. As already mentioned they do create a lot of dust – both coarse and fine. I now do my heavy-duty shaping outside on fine days only – preferably when there is a

breeze! Two or three days in the garden in early autumn can produce enough stock to cover a winter's carving. Despite using the Lords dust extractor I still wear a face mask for this task.

Some carvers who make extensive use of grinding burrs have a work table which has a mesh top over a collection hopper. The bottom of the hopper is connected to a dust and chip extractor. Although I have the large collector coupled to my turning lathes I find the reassurance of a solid wooden work-bench or leather-aproned thighs too 'comfortable' to give up. Hence I rely on an air-swept breathing mask. As a result I am now made to remove all top clothing before being allowed into the house! If I didn't the chips would really fly!

— 6 —

GETTING INTO SHAPE

Where does 'roughing' end and 'final shaping' begin? In fact there is no clear dividing line – not even, necessarily, a change of process. If you have created the rough shape with a coarse ¼in Kutzall burr you will have raised the wood to a fluffy torn surface, but the profile could be close to the required final shape and dimensions. Now you switch to an ⅛in Kutzall and then on to a Ruby burr. Working through these will give you a very smooth finish and your bird could be ready to have the feathers carved. You have just seamlessly moved through the various stages of shaping.

If, on the other hand, you have carved the blank with chisel and mallet, knife, and spokeshave, there is a much clearer distinction – you now have to take up the fine burrs or abrasive paper to smooth out the tool marks.

Today, as far as most bird carvers are concerned, more of the detail shaping is done with power-driven burrs rather than with carving tools. There are also areas where you need to use small saws and carving chisels and gouges. Certainly the American 'tradition' now leans heavily towards using burrs for most tasks on decoy carving.

However, many of us find that it is much more satisfying to cut rather than to tear wood with a burr. At almost every stage either approach will achieve the results you require until you come to the final smoothing down. When finishing, power methods win hands down. Of course burrs make a lot of dust and this may condition your choice. Equally there are long lines and hollow areas such as around beaks, pouches and under wingtips which are naturals for carving gouges.

In shaping with powered burrs – both coarse carbide and the fine diamond and rubies – you can almost totally ignore the grain. With power and large blade edge tools, and even later with the small palm tool detailing gouges, you have to be much more careful about the direction of cutting. First there is the obvious problem of breakout. If you get under the ends of fibres and apply too much pressure, large splinters can break away. Frequently you have to mark out the limit of the cut that you wish to make with a stop cut. This may be a cross-grain vertical incision with a chisel, or even a small saw cut. As you get down to the fine detail the cut may first be marked out by burning the line with a pyrograph, and the burn mark may itself be the 'stop cut'.

With edge tools there are really three things to try to avoid.

1. Do not cut along the grain into rising grain.
2. Do not work across end grain towards an open face
3. Do not cut a channel, step edge or raised profile without first defining the edges.

Powered burrs are not so sensitive, but you can see a distinct difference in finish with coarse burrs when used *against* the rotation as this raises considerable fluffy tearing.

To explore these ideas we will be working through the carving of a feather-

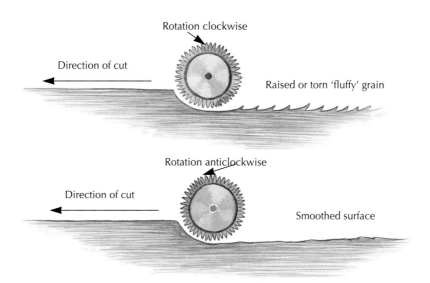

Fluffy torn grain by using coarse burrs against the direction of rotation.

detailed bird – a duck in a standard pose with beak straight forward, and a flat base set at waterline depth. It is a one-piece blank which has now been carved to the correct overall dimensions.

You have already decided what 'set' or posture of wings and tail that you require. Let's say that the wingtips are crossed and the tail is in the relaxed position – that is, turned down.

You have been working to an elevation and plan drawing but may or may not have a front view or sections (many plans books do not provide these).

Although the outline profile of your carving seen in silhouette looks fine and corresponds with the plan, the bird in your hands probably looks lumpy and not right.

If you do have a front view on your plans (and have even made a section template), you will see a distinct hollowing where the wings are lying on the side of the body. The wings tuck into a definite 'pouch'. This runs (faintly) from the top of the body a short distance behind the neck, and round in a sweep where the front of the folded wings lie. It then deepens as it runs along the side of the

body, and then shallows again as it sweeps up towards the top of the front of the tail. A section template will show a clear indentation about half-way down the sides at the widest part of the body. It is very rare in real life that the edge of the wing is clearly defined unless the bird is in a tense displaying or calling posture. Normally the wings are folded into the pouch feathers and the top of the fold is hidden under the scapulars. In my carvings, however, the edges of the folded wings are often outlined to make them more distinctive.

On the top of the bird, running down the centre of the back, there will be a trough where the two wings almost meet. With a soft carpenter's pencil, shade in the wing outline and the various hollows. This is an area where you may first shape with a gouge before working with burrs to smooth the curves and slopes and cut any required hard edges. If you have a section template check the widest area profile. If not, you can measure off from your drawings and then test with a pair of large external calipers.

The next areas to work up are the

Full rest

Wings tucked into side pockets
No clear wing line can be seen

Semi display or
preparing for flight

Wings held off the body
There is a clear edge to the wing

The profile through the side pouches.

wingtips and the tail. From the plan and elevation views trace on the top and the sides, the outline of the tail and the wingtip feathers. Here you will have to use some judgement. The drawings will show only the silhouette profiles – these do not help in determining the degree of overlap at the crossing point, neither do they show the side-to-side set or angle of the feathers.

At this stage you will probably find that there is some waste to be cut away under the wingtips and over the tail. Use a saw – either a small tennon or a coping saw are ideal – and then gouges to complete the broad outline. For most carvings it is best to work the wingtips first and gradually move down to the tail.

Wings can be set into one of a number of postures. Most are variants of two patterns. In one, the one we have chosen, the wingtips are crossed. In the other standard posture the primary feathers lie straight along the back, with the primaries almost parallel to each other.

Remember that whatever the overall stance, the wings are lying on the top *and the sides* of the body. The primary feathers that protrude furthest at the back rarely lie absolutely flat along the top of the bird. These long feathers that are rising up from the side pouches, are naturally lying at a slight side-to-side slope, whether they are crossed or open. When crossed the ends are usually standing a little proud of the body itself, and the primaries lie more

Checking the dimensions of the hollow under the wings using large callipers.

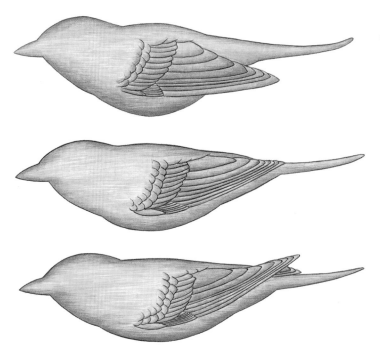

towards the top of the bird. The tips are then often turned up slightly and look much better if, on the carving, the lift is exaggerated.

When the wingtips are not crossed, the primaries will obviously be a little lower and are more likely to lie flat on the body.

In your carving, it is the vulnerability of these projecting primary tips that will lead us later to consider carving the primaries separately as feather inserts.

With the main shapes of the wing ends drawn on, you will find that there will be some substantial timber removal required on a cross-winged posture. To shape the area around the crossing and under the raised tips, a long straight, medium-grit Kutzall is a good bet.

There are a number of options for the tail posture. Basically the feathers can be pulled in close to give a simple rounded or even a pointed end. Alternatively the feathers are spread into more of a fan.

There are then three stances. In the fully relaxed position such as the one that we are working on, the feathers are drawn together and run straight out horizontally from the body. The sides of the tail turn down so that the edge feathers are lower than those in the centre.

The spread tail can be almost flat or turned up so that the edge feathers are higher than those at the centre. In extreme you get a distinctly cocked-up profile as on the Robin or Wren. In the duck world there are some where, in display, the tail sticks up like an aircraft braking flap – or more prosaically, a Peacock's fan. The Ruddy Duck is one of these (*see* the diagram on page 84).

Eventually you reach the stage where the outlines of the wings and the tail have been rough carved and have then been more precisely defined and shaped. Next move to the head end.

All species of bird have head structures

that are unique to the type. Ducks' heads are longer front to back than other birds, but even within the duck family the variations are enormous. Owls have round heads with 'pushed in' faces. Birds of prey vary widely, but many have very round heads with streamlined cheeks and distinctive heavy eyebrows.

The cheeks of ducks sweep back in an almost continuous curve from the beak. When calling, their cheeks puff out. There are several birds that have tufts, and ruffs, and other head feather patterns that are distinctive, and that stick out well beyond the skeletal profile. Few plans provide sufficient information on the details of each of these variations, and simply drawn outlines can be very misleading; it is here that a small library of bird books soon becomes essential.

At best your plans will have indicated that the head is not fully rounded but that there is a hollowing of the face above the cheek, but accurate sections through the face are rarely shown. In your workshop you should have at least one Study Head. These are plaster mouldings of the heads of real birds and the fine detail gives essential insights into eyes, beaks, and the general bumps and hollows.

The beak certainly requires a level of detailing that goes beyond the information provided on most plans. Here our study head really comes into its own. Obviously it would be very nice to have a head for each variety of bird that you want to carve, but the cost would be horrendous. One duck's head will give you detail that with a little adaptation will look reasonably authentic on most other species of duck. Bill profiles vary

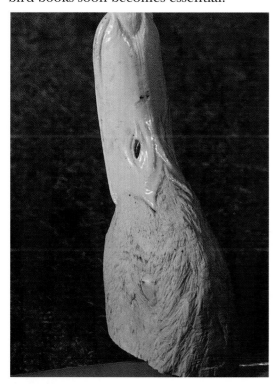

A study bill showing the level of detail that is possible.

The underside of the bill. The broken area shows the depth of undercutting and the detail of the lamella.

enormously from bird to bird, but given an outline profile, one or two study heads and some hard observation, you can with care produce reasonably accurate results.

Until you have really examined a study head or the beak of a real bird, you will not begin to understand the detail required under the beak and the extent of the surface undulations.

The initial shaping of the beak, head and neck may be accomplished with a small draw-knife, but access to the required line is often very difficult, and therefore most of the basic head shaping is done with medium and then fine burrs. Round-ended and tapered burrs feature widely. We will be returning to the detailing of beaks in the next chapter when we look at feather burning.

I do not drill the eye sockets until the facial structure has been finally shaped, and do not indent the eyelids until the eye socket has been drilled.

External calipers are very useful in establishing the position for drilling the eye holes. Even if you do not have a good enough drawing to establish the setting for the calipers, they can be opened to the correct gap on the blank and then by viewing from above and a full frontal position you can ensure that the eyes are level and equally distant from the beak and so forth. With the position fixed, a circle of the diameter of the socket is drawn on each side of the face.

Drill a pilot hole in the centre of the mark. By drilling deep from each side the two pilots will meet in the middle of the head. In my case the holes are not drilled out to full eye diameter, as I prefer to hollow out a chamber with a small milling cutter. The lip of the chamber is then worked out to the finished diameter – using a glass eye to test it. Do not fix the eyes in place yet.

So the finished shape has been achieved and is as smooth as you can get it with chisels and burrs. The problem is

that small burrs, in particular, leave furrows, bumps and tiny hollows, some of which only become visible when viewed under oblique light. Unfortunately they become blindingly obvious when you incise the feather barbs.

You will probably find that some sanding or filing has become essential. A set of riffler files of various profiles and sections will help you to get in along the edges of feathers. Constantly check the surface under oblique light. You are not trying to make it grain smooth – that is unnecessary; but you do want to get rid of bumps and hollows.

Power sanders can be used to achieve an even and smoother finish. Tiny sanding discs run at slow speeds on your mini grinder can sharpen up detail. If you are using hand-held abrasive papers then a hard rubber sanding block is a good investment. Some carvers have made up sets of miniature blocks with hard and medium rubber and foam faces in various shapes and contours. The abrasives are sometimes glued on, but most are held onto the pads by hand. The different profiles and softness of the blocks allow them to get hard up against an edge, work into corners, and cover concave and convex surfaces.

For initial sanding, the 2in diameter

Using a pair of calipers to fix the position of the eye sockets.

The main feather group areas are marked off on the carved blank. It is at this stage that great care is taken to get maximum symmetry side to side.

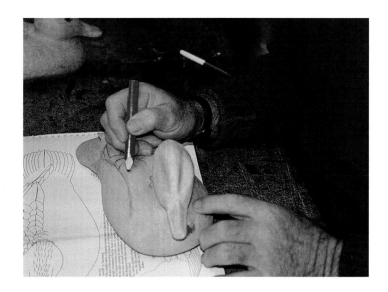

Velcro-backed sanding disc devices much loved by turners are effective, and some of the new multi-profile power detail sanders are extremely useful. Start with 240 grit and move on to 400. The Velcro sanders are better run on a flexible drive to give the control needed to work detail. It is impossible to manipulate a ¼in drill with a directly mounted sander on anything as small and intricate as a bird carving. Standard drum sanders and flap wheels are far too crude and aggressive.

The final stage is to go over the whole bird with fine abrasive paper held in the hand without a sanding block. It may seem a little odd to be spending this level of effort getting a really smooth finish if, in a few moments, you are going to carve all over it, but any imperfections or blemishes on the evenness of the surface will show later – particularly on a polished wood finished bird or a flat painted slick.

Most carvers now draw on all the feather outlines. If your original drawings or templates show all the details of the feathers you can measure off from the plans and accurately establish key points. If not you may have to work from photographs or artists' impressions in bird books.

Start by tracing in soft pencil, constantly checking the view from the front, top, and side to ensure that you are getting an appropriate level of both size and positional symmetry between the sides.

It is very easy to make mistakes. First outline the main areas. Indicate where breast feathers end and wings start. Mark covert zones and then primaries. Draw the position of the junction between tail and body feathers. Make sure you have side-to-side symmetry of the zone locations.

Next, starting from the front and working towards the back and from the top down the sides, draw in the outline of each feather. Constantly remind yourself that you are drawing the feathers of a bird that flies *forward*. This is not as silly as it sounds. Feathers overlap like the tiles on a roof. Get the overlap wrong and the wind would get under the feather and lift it up like an air brake.

The trailing edge of one feather will always overlap the leading edge of the following or lower feathers. Down the centre of the breast the two sides meet and both sides of the central feather will overlap those either side of it.

The feathers on the leading edge of the

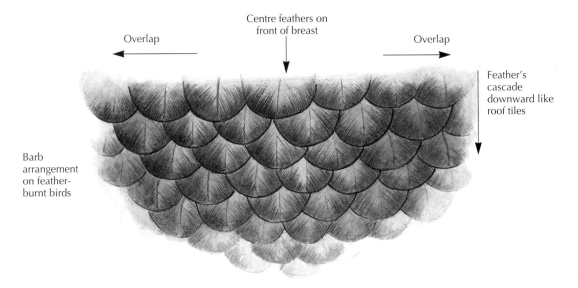

The arrangement of feathers adopted for the breast. Note the direction of overlap – it differs from one side to the other.

wings are small – in fact some are tiny – and they increase considerably in size towards the trailing edge. Those at the top of the neck are small and size increases as you move down the breast. Similarly there is a gradation down the side of the body.

My drawings start in soft pencil since mistakes can be rubbed or sanded off and redrawn. Once satisfactory they are over-traced in biro. The ink will withstand a lot more handling and the carving is certainly going to get a lot of that in the next stage. The ink marks will of course disappear as soon as we start detail carving.

With the feather profiles drawn we have another techniques choice point. For me edge tools come into their own. First the outline of each feather is incised using a fine vee gouge. I aim for a near vertical edge to the feather by tipping the gouge slightly. At this stage I prefer not to undercut the feathers but to leave them at full thickness until I am satisfied that all are correct.

Ashley Isles now produce a trio of small, palm tools that are particularly useful.

Two are micro vee gouges, one spoon and one back bent, and the other is a scimitar profiled cutting tool to a design by carver Ray Gonzales. This is particularly useful for chamfering the steps of the over-lapping feathers.

The vee outlining does make an incision that is unrealistically deep. (Remember how difficult it was to see the edges of feathers on a real bird.) Don't worry about this as a little overall light sanding will reduce each feather to a small 'mound' which is quite realistic. When working the breast feathers the vee cut is kept quite shallow. The back and side pouch feathers are incised deeper, and the wing and tail feathers are cut deepest of all.

The alternative adopted by many carvers is to outline all feathers using a pyrograph. The pyrograph approach is quick and easy but it has one disadvantage. You need a tough burning tip – the Detailmaster tool described in Chapter 10 is ideal. With this held vertical to the surface and at full heat, the outline of each feather is deeply incised. To get the penetration required some force is applied and the tool is moved slowly.

The problem with the outline burning approach is that it produces a permanent hard burnt and even line around each feather. This looks artificial if it is not going to be painted over. If you examine the feathers on a real bird you will see two things. First the actual outlines of the feathers are often difficult to detect – until you look very closely one appears to merge or blur into the next. The second thing that you will notice is that the edges of feathers are not continuous but there are frequent breaks of various sizes, and the edges are often quite ragged.

It is in the process of preening that the barbs all come together and the feather is re-formed – but they do not remain in that state for very long. So to make your bird look realistic you need to break up the outline of the feathers with 'feather breaks'. If your feathers have a burnt outline this is not so easy to achieve. Therefore many of us prefer to carve the outlines with a vee gouge and then to create the step with chisel, knife or burr.

Following either the burning or the vee gouge outlining, the root of the under-lying feather is chamfered to provide a step which will be worked to simulate an exaggerated overlay. For cutting these chamfers, chisels are often preferred to rotary burrs as they give a more even 'cut'.

The step effect is now cut around all feathers and the feather edges and corners are cleaned up. For cleaning up, a tapered diamond burr is a good starting point. The problem is that you can not always get in to some corners and recesses, and it is not always easy to get a straight line along the edge of a primary feather. So we now need to call in another carver's friend – one or more riffler files. As mentioned earlier, rifflers come in many shapes, flat and round, straight and cranked, and a small set is a useful adjunct to your tool-kit.

We have not yet, however, finished with the edges. In most instances you will wish to do a little 'relieving'. Some carvers exaggerate the edges of the larger feathers to make them stand off from the feathers that they overlay. This is the process known as 'relieving' the feathers. In some cases the step and undercutting will be heavy enough to make the edge of the overlapping feather stand visibly clear of the one underneath; in others the relieving is minimal just to make the edge feather-like.

Again you have a choice of method.

A favourite group of working tools. The chisels and gouges are by Crown, and the small palm vee tools are by Ashley Isles. These latter get used so much for feather detailing that they have already worn down and been replaced.

Outline feathers with Vee gouge

Deepest cut with Vee gouge laid over

Shoulder cut away with flat chisel

Final Vee cut with side of gouge laid flat

Rounding feather with flat chisel

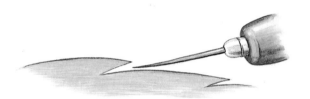

Deep under-cutting with fine diamond burr

Shaping the feathers.

Underburning with a pyrograph can be very effective. Still deeper relieving starts with a small pointed diamond burr and is probably completed with a very fine straight burr. While you are doing this the burr is lifted every so often so that it breaks up through the feather edge to create the 'breaks'. Alternatively the breaks can be burnt from above with the pyro tool.

The final stage in outlining the feathers is to get the overall appearance right. If you require a more dramatic effect with each feather clearly defined against its neighbour your final sanding will be relatively light leaving a clear step at the edge of each feather. If on the other hand you want the feathers more rounded with each almost blending into the one it overlies, then there will be more sanding

to do. Work along the grain from neck towards tail starting with 180 grit abrasive. Carry on through to 400 grit.

The bird is now ready to have the actual texture of the feathers burnt or carved on. Amongst the ranks of carvers you will find many different styles. Some go for as near perfect a replication of real feathers as possible; others go for a far more impressionistic approach.

There is a popular style in which the feathers are not exactly replicated in that the center quill is not defined and the individual barbs are only loosely simulated by slightly exaggerated fore and aft gouging. Here the feather edges are usually relieved. This is the style that is widely used as the base for realistic colour washes and detail painting. The effect can

This duck has been gouged with a milling cutter and will later be painted.

The stones and milling cutters used to create a feather effect suitable for painting.

A feather-burnt Pintail in natural surroundings.

look quite good. It is certainly very much quicker to do than are some of the more fully representational approaches.

The next approach is another popular style that is very effective but is exceedingly time-consuming. Many of the carved examples in this book employ this method. Here the feathers are individually carved but in a somewhat stylized way. The quill is shown and the barbs radiate out from this (probably at a slightly more acute angle than they do in reality). After outline carving and relieving, the feathers – including each barb – are burnt with a pyrograph tool. When complete the bird is oiled and is left uncoloured. The brown coloration produced by the burning looks very like the plumage of many a hen bird.

While each of the feather-working processes have particular techniques of their own, there are some common basic practices, and many carvers mix and remix the approaches.

Have you been watching the clock? Bird carving is not a quick process. It probably took you only 10–15 minutes to mark out the block and band-saw to a shaped blank. Carving it to a finished shape may have taken 2–4 hours – much longer for a more complicated bird; but since then the clock has been racing. You may well have spent a whole day developing the outlines of the feathers even on a simple standard pose. Step carving and relieving has swallowed another day. An owl with raised wings will take me one or two weeks to develop the feather structure before a single barb can be burnt.

The next stage of texturing the feathers is a half- to five-day process. But please don't give up, what you have now produced is beginning to look interesting.

FEATHERS AND ALL!

Before we do any further work on the bird, let's think about what it is that we are trying to achieve. In the last chapter we talked broadly about different styles of representing feathers, we now need to look at this subject in much more detail.

We have three starting considerations. First we have to always remember that we are working with wood not feathers, so the material, with its own characteristics, introduces very clear constraints. Secondly we will find that the different feathers in each of the various anatomical zones – the 'groups' on a bird – have their own unique characteristics.

The third point is that whatever level of realism we are aiming for, what we actually do is to go for the broadest acceptable levels of impressionism. We will, at best, mark off and 'carve' only a couple of hundred or so feather representations. In reality even the smallest duck will have many many times that number. We can, of course, only show those that lie on the surface; on a real bird there are many layers of overlap. We will show, say, breast feathers as being a centimetre or so long. In life you actually only see a fraction of a millimetre tip of each of the overlapping feathers. We often carve a quill. In reality you only see a small part of the quills on just a few of the larger wing feathers. We grossly exaggerate the feather breaks, which again are rarely apparent on casual observation. We do not go for absolute detail on beaks, around eyes, or on the feet. In other words we exercise very considerable 'artistic licence'.

On feather-detailed birds that are not to be painted the feathers are emphasized to clearly show the structure, the breaks are exaggerated to get away from artificial

The feather definition on this Owl is made a little clearer by colour rather than an obvious outline.

The feathers have been drawn on and are now being outlined with a micro vee gouge.

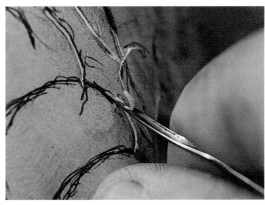

Developing the feather profiles.
1) Marking the outline – micro vee gouge.

2) Cutting away the overlap – flat fish tail chisel.

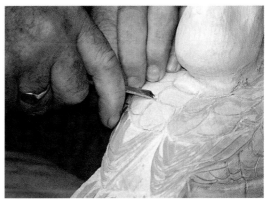

3) Cleaning into the corners – flat skew cutter.

4) Outlining the tail feathers – bent micro vee.

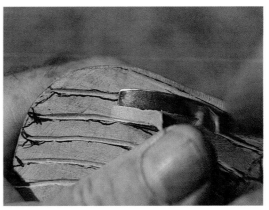

Making the step – bent chisel.

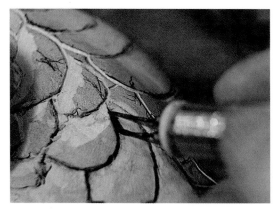

The burning alternative.
1) Undercutting with a hard tipped pyro tool.

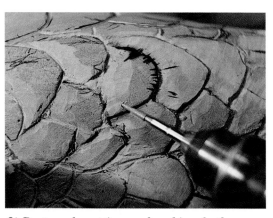

2) Deep undercutting and making feather breaks.

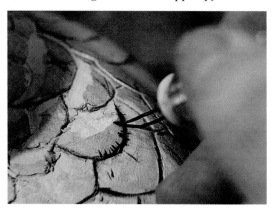

3) Burning in the feather breaks.

4) Deep burning under the wings.

5) The burnt feathers ready for rounding.

outlines around our stylized feathers. Fundamentally we are portraying structure, and we are demonstrating (and selling) our artistic, interpretive and craft skills. The detail on a real duck is so fine that we do not have the tools or skills with which to replicate it. Getting a totally exact representation would require that we used fibres not blocks of wood, and it would probably take a lifetime for us to complete a reasonable-sized bird.

Of course with polished natural wood carvings we are looking for the broad sweeping overall shape or form, and here we are even more impressionistic. We often smooth out ripples and indentations along major curves and emphasize the sweeping line. We may also give only a hint of the wing position and a smidgen of an idea of the tail feathers.

When we are preparing a carving for painting we may no longer be so concerned with the structure of the feathers. If we are going for realism, we want our bird to have the natural undulations that a multi-layered feathered surface would have, but beyond this we are very impressionistic in our representations of the barbs of the feathers. If, on the other hand we are going for the stylized representation of the Slick – as in the cheap and cheerful Chinese imports – or our more skilful feather-stroke painted variety, we want as smooth and blemish-free a surface as possible. Now the carving is merely a beautifully prepared canvas on which we will apply our colour.

Whether we are making a feather-carved or a painted bird, one thing is certain, we need to know something of feather structures and patterns. So far we have been copying the information given in plans. The results will be OK – for the time being!

Improving the results is not so much a matter of skill, but rather more of understanding. Once we fully realize what it is that we are trying to represent you will see huge improvements. We have all seen plenty of feathers and handled many, but it is often not until you look at them with an eye to reproducing them that you become wholly aware of two fundamentals.

First no feather, whatever light it is seen in, is completely one solid, even colour. A 'pure' white feather will have bluey-grey light-cast shadows. A black feather will have lights of blue and green, and sometimes an iridescence.

Secondly, although many feathers have a clear organized colour pattern and all the feathers in a group have broadly similar markings and appearance – no two feathers of a bird are ever identical. Even two that are side by side can be unbelievably different. The spots may be in a different place on adjacent feathers; a colour patch may start in the middle of one, run right across the next two or three, and then finish half way across the fourth. Some birds, such as the Loon, have a pattern of markings which looks totally unnatural and quite bizarre. The Loon has diagonal rows of almost square small patches of white running right across the black back. Many birds have totally 'random' dots scattered over a different body colour.

The third factor is that the texture and structure of feathers differ enormously from one group of birds to another.

Earlier it was recommended that you build up a collection of feathers as you walked the marshes, fields and parks. It is

The tips of the wing feathers on the trailing edge are very fragile, and often run across the grain. These would be better if made individually and fixed in as inserts.

75

probable that most of the collection will be of wing feathers – these are the ones that are most likely to fall from the bird. If you go to waterside areas where birds spend time preening you may also get some body and the occasional tail feathers. Determining where on the bird the feathers come from is not easy. The feathers you pick up will look very different from those on a bird. The reason is that, like icebergs, only a small part of each feather is normally visible.

If you look at one breast feather in isolation – the one we represent as a centimetre in length – it is probably 3cm or 4cm in length and it will naturally have a shaft or quill – in this case central. The whiskers or barbs which make up the feather will shoot out sideways from the quill. Also at the base will be a bunch of fluffy fibres or down. When you look at the same feather on the breast you will see only the tip, probably less than a couple of millimeters of the whole feather, and you certainly will not see any of the down. Of the tip that you see the barbs will sometimes appear to be almost parallel to each other, and certainly do not look as though they are radiating out from a central shaft.

Similarly the feathers on the pouch have very fine and extremely flexible barbs; they are quite long and have a tuft of down at the base.

The barbs on the softer feathers do lock together but the interlock is not a strong one; hence there are many more breaks. The feathers look 'untidy' and less formal. Obviously it is these much softer, more downy feathers that are used for stuffing pillows and cushions.

Wing feathers are very different. They have to support the bird in flight and to withstand considerable wind pressure and buffeting. They must, therefore, be strong. This means that they need a good, unyielding, central spine – the quill. Writing quills used by medieval scholars were cut from the primary feathers of large birds (usually geese or swans). The barbs, also strong and stiff, radiate out at an angle from the shaft, and having a Velcro-like edge structure they lock together quite firmly – they need to withstand the wind pressure of flight. When the wings are folded the feathers stack up on each other – in flight they are spread out and much more of each wing feather can be seen.

It is very difficult to see any defined shapes to the feathers on this stuffed Grouse. Any feather-burnt representation would therefore need to be very impressionistic.

A Pheasant's wing and a multi-banded feather. It is difficult to capture these effects without colour.

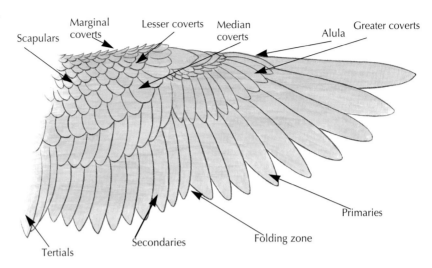

The arrangement of wing feathers and the named groups.

Scapulars · Marginal coverts · Lesser coverts · Median coverts · Alula · Greater coverts · Primaries · Folding zone · Secondaries · Tertials

Most teachers of bird carving recommend not only the building of a collection of feathers, but they also suggest that you practise on offcuts of timber the carving and burning, or drawing and colouring of single feathers and then whole feather groups.

Understanding some of the basics we can now look at the different feathers and consider how they may be replicated.

THE WING FEATHERS

There are nine different feather zones on the top of the wings, and six are then nominally repeated under the wings. The feathers along the whole trailing edge of the wing are only a single layer, so they are shared top and underside. On the top of the wing, right beside the body on the trailing edge are a small group of tightly overlapping feathers, the Tertials. Next to these and going half way out along the wing top to where it folds are the Secondaries. From this point out to the wingtip are the Primaries. The Primaries are long, usually taper to a near point and, relative to their length, are often narrow.

The shapes of the feathers in these three wing groups vary more from species to species of bird, than do the rest of the wing feathers. On Owls the primaries are much broader and rounded at the tip. For all birds the one or two feathers at the extreme wingtip are more tapered and pointed than are the other primaries.

Most secondaries are long and straight with rounded tips while the tertials (of which little is ever seen when the wings are folded) are most frequently almond-shaped.

When the wings are folded it is the primaries that extend furthest along towards, and even overlapping, the tail, but most of their length is covered by the now overlying secondaries. As we saw much earlier the outer section of the wing folds in under the inner. Both are then covered by the Coverts. For practical purposes it is best to think that the 'wings' fold in under the coverts. This means that the longer Greater Coverts go furthest along the body, and it is these that you see when you look down on a swimming duck. Then as you move towards the head, first the medium-length Median Coverts overlie the Greater, then the Lesser Coverts lie on top of the Medians. Finally, sweeping up to the neck you get the much finer Scapulars.

77

The feather arrangement on the top of a Garganney.

The shapes of the coverts are very species specific. On some birds they are blunter and almost square-ended – particularly the greaters. On most birds they are rounded or almond-shaped, but on some, such as the Garganney, they are very long, fine, tapering to a point, and may even droop down over the side of the body when the duck is at rest.

The Marginal Coverts at the front edge of the wing are often very tiny even on quite large birds, but these all disappear under body feathers when the wings are folded.

Not quite half way along the leading edge of the wing there is a joint which bulges a little forward of the wing line. This is covered by a small group of feathers known as the Alula. They lie at the outer end of the row of median coverts and are a little larger.

If the wings are folded you will not be interested in the layout of the underwing feathers. However there will come a time when you wish to carve a bird in flight, or more likely stretching with the wings up exposing the full underside.

Covering the crease where the underwing joins the body is a row of long, very soft feathers known as the Axillars. There are two points to remember when laying out the feathers. Whatever the posture, the feathers rapidly increase in size from the leading to the training edge of the wing, and each 'row' of feathers decreases in size along the length towards the wingtip with the specific exceptions of the

The tiny and indefinite feathers on the leading edge of the wing of a Buzzard.

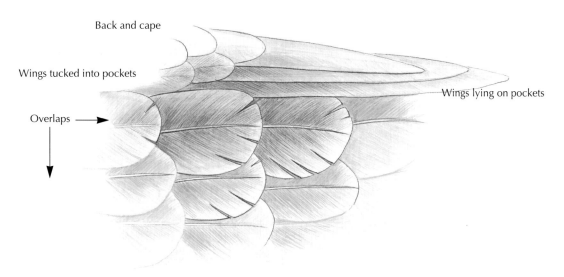

Back and cape

Wings tucked into pockets

Wings lying on pockets

Overlaps →

The feather overlaps on side pouches.

primaries and secondaries that get larger towards the tip. The second feature to be sure that you get right is that the leading edge of each feather overlies the one in front of it. When seen from underneath the position is obviously reversed. Now the trailing edge of the feather overlies the leading edge of the one behind it

All of this holds whether the primaries are crossed or open on a squatting bird. About a fifth of the wing area has a skeleton and flesh substructure. All of the wing feathers are rooted in and sustained by this. Those directly supported by it do not need the strength of the unsupported flight feathers. Hence the coverts are smaller and softer with a much less well-defined quill.

On all feathers the barbs radiate out from the quill. At the base of every feather there is a small tuft of down, but once you get beyond this the barbs stick out to the side. The first few barbs leave the quill almost at right angles. They have a slight curve on them so that the end of the barb bends a little towards the feather's tip. As you move along the feather, the barb to quill angle gradually reduces. In the last centimetre or so the angle changes rapidly

until the last few barbs are almost straight back continuations of the quill.

Note: before you buy a pyrograph to burn feathers please read the information on burners in the Chapter 10 on tools, in your enthusiasm you can easily get it very wrong!

In burning a primary feather we emphasize both the well-defined nature of the barbs by burning more deeply, and their strong line by making the burn straight or only slightly curved. Start at the first exposure of the feather near the root end. Use a broad chisel-ended pyro tip and start at the quill, making a strong line out towards the edge of the feather. You will not be starting at that part of the feather where in reality the barbs would be almost at right angles to the quill so the angle of the burn line will be somewhere near 70 degrees.

The first burn will establish the line for the rest of the barbs so make it carefully. By starting at the quill the hot iron will burn slightly harder (deeper and giving a darker colour). As the pyro tip moves across the surface of the wood it cools slightly so that the burn becomes less intense the longer the stroke. This gives a

79

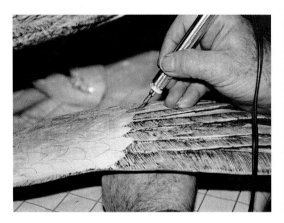

Burning in the feather detail.
1) Hand steadied to get good parallel lines.

2) Undercutting an edge. The burner is
designed to keep cool despite the close grip.

3) Burning small pouch and flank feathers.

nice gradation of colour to the feathers. Like the hair on a 'bottle blond' you can see the dark roots!

By holding the pyro between index finger and thumb, as you would a pen, you can control the stroke by a flexing of the two digits. The fleshy part of the lower side of the hand can now rest on the carving to steady it. After making two or three strokes you slide your hand gently sideways. With a little practice you can build up skills which allow you to get each stroke close to the side of and exactly paralleling the previous one. If the burning process is not to become hugely time-consuming and very boring then you do need to develop speed and an even and regular movement.

Change the angle of the barb line slightly between each adjacent feather to avoid a continuous barb running from one side of the bird to the other.

The coverts are not burned overall quite so hard as the primaries although the margin of overlay is one of the areas where we typically undercut to define the edge of the greater coverts. Median and lesser coverts are then burnt lighter still and the edges are kept more diffuse.

When the wings are folded onto the back we do not see much of the lesser coverts as most are hidden under the Scapulars and the Cape. Most of what you see on the top of the upper back are the scapulars that are usually quite large feathers. As you move up towards the neck

Various feathers – note the multiple breaks on the breast feathers.

A St James's Pintail. This bird, in beautiful spring condition, shows the strong vermiculations on the cape and the softer lines on the pouches.

A Pintail's back showing the long dark and the fine vermiculated cape feathers.

you reach the area that is known as the Cape. Again on some birds the cape may consist of long, narrow, pointed feathers. These are the feathers that fishermen use for the hackles of the flies that they tie.

The scapular feathers, particularly the long narrow ones, have barbs that are swept back from the quill at a very shallow angle. They are soft, 'feathery', and the velcro bond is much weaker.

THE POCKETS

Before leaving the wings we need to return to the question of posture. Earlier we identified two patterns; in one the tips of the wings were crossed and the primaries probably stood proud of the body and had a slight rise at the outer end. In the second at-rest posture the wings lie flat on the body in a straight fore and aft alignment. These are the only two postures we use on birds in the standard 'swimming' or squatting poses. If you observe birds that are standing or walking you will often see a third posture – watch the Blackbird feeding in your garden. Here the wingtips are not crossed and the wings though lying on the body are held lower so that they make a diagonal line down the side of the body and the primaries droop down below the tail – almost as though they were dragging. This stance provides an interesting bit of extra detail on a standing bird.

The side of the body has a zone of large, broader and softer feathers that form what is called the Pocket. When the bird is at rest with the wings folded, the leading edge of the outer section of the wing is usually tucked into the top of the pocket, hence the line of the top of the pocket feathers may be higher than the line of the bulge caused by the underlying wings. This is not always the case and even at rest you may see a bird with the wings resting on top of the pocket. Certainly for me a carving with the wings lapping over the pocket feathers is a little more interesting as you then have a strong line down the side of the bird. For blanks being prepared for feather-stroke painting however, it is much easier to opt for the style where the wings overlap the pockets.

The pocket starts at the front of the flanks just forward of the shoulder (the knuckle where the Alula feathers are). Here the feathers are relatively small. As you work back along the body the pocket feathers increase in size quite considerably. On some birds they are quite rounded while on others they have a giant almond profile.

In life their outlines are ill-defined. Because they are so soft, they lie very flat and the edges are difficult to detect. They are also very prolific, so very little of the tip of a feather protrudes beyond the tip of the one that overlies it.

On some birds such as the Mallard hen they are more widely spaced and each feather is colour banded so that when the hen is sitting it looks like a cluster of fallen leaves. Seen out in the open this patterning makes the shape of the feathers quite distinctive.

In our impression of pouch feathers we burn them to appear large, distinctive and well-defined. In preparing the carving for realistic painted feathering on the other hand, we may not incise them quite so strongly but merely work the whole surface of the bird with little semi-circles of fine burr gouged lines.

Note that the lower edge of each pocket feather overlaps the top of the feather below it – and, of course, the whole feather overlaps the one behind it. As already identified the top of the pocket may overlap the wings or disappear under them. Your choice!

THE BREAST

The normal portrayal of the breast feathers shows these as a little like a tiled roof. There is however an important difference.

Detail study of Barn Owl showing the structure of the eye area. Note again the soft ill-defined feathers of the breast – these are particularly important to silent flight.

To give the soft effect of the breast feathers the wood is roughened with a medium/coarse burr, and a few feather-like burnt incisions are made.

The similarities are that the feathers cascade downwards with the upper ones overlapping those below; and that the centre of the upper tile lies above the joint between the two immediately below – just as do tiles on a roof.

The key difference is that in a horizontal row of roofing tiles the tiles abut each other, whereas on a bird the breast feathers also overlap in this plane as well. Starting at the centre of the front of the breast and moving sideways the feather always overlaps the edge of the one behind it. Hence the centre feather overlaps on both sides and then, as you move round, the trailing edge of each feather lies on top of the leading edge of the next. As you are drawing the feather outlines on, it is very easy to make a mistake. A slip does not matter very much here, but if you do not notice and continue with the wrong overlap on into the pockets then the error becomes much more obvious.

The normal method of burning breast feathers is to create little half moons with no quill showing and 'soft' strokes radiating out round the moon. Whether you clearly outline the feathers and/or undercut them in any way is up to you depending on how much you wish to veer towards the dramatic.

Tail feathers with central quill and angled barbs

Note rump feathers similar to breast but 'rising' overlaps

Feather arrangement on the underside of the rump and tail.

Various tail postures.

The breast feathers of live ducks are often more distinctive and clearly defined than they are on some other species of birds that need to be less 'waterproof'. Birds that rely on silent flight for the catching of prey have particularly soft body feathers. The breasts of owls and birds of prey (especially hawks) appear at first glance to have whiskers rather than feathers. Of course they are feathers, but they have very diffuse outlines and tips. In simulating these all you need to do is to first raise the surface to a fluffy texture with a medium grit Kutzall and then burn small clusters of faint radiating barbs. The lighter and more sparse the burning, the better the impression.

THE TAIL AREA

Here there are three zones that we need to consider. The first is the top of the bird to the front of the main tail feathers. Some of this area is seen under the ends of the wings. When the wingtips are crossed there is also a small window of back feathers just in front of the crossing. All the feathers in this zone are small and

downy becoming only slightly larger as you near the tail. They are best dealt with as tiny breast feathers. They really do not need out-lining as this would only give them distracting prominence.

The body feathers under the tail are just a little stronger in definition, and are again best treated in the same way as are breast feathers. There is a difference however. Breast feathers clearly cascade from the neck straight down; the under-tail feathers are a continuation of a sweep from the side pockets gradually sweeping upwards to the underside of the butt ends of the tail feathers. Here those from the two sides meet in the middle in a rising overlap. They are soft and normally have ill-defined outlines.

The tail feathers themselves are usually long, narrow, and similar to small editions of the primaries in their structure and characteristics. Again they have a distinct central quill. The ends may be pointed, rounded, or squared off according to species. Hovering birds tend more to broader tail feathers each with a near square end.

When we were discussing overall posture in marking out the blank for sawing, we identified some basic patterns. Different birds display in different ways – some, the Peacock and the Ruddy Duck for example, raise and spread their tail feathers in a form of fan. Blackbirds and Robins expressing anger or aggression cock the tail up but do not fan. Some ducks, in what could be a display, half cock the tail so than the feathers spread in a semi fan, the tip of the tail is higher that the front and the two side edges are inclined upwards. In repose the tail slopes downwards and it may be almost flat or turned down slightly at the sides. In most repose positions the feathers are drawn together.

In burning these patterns, the greater the degree of displaying the more you will see of the quill of each feather, and the deeper the level of undercutting to exaggerate the overlap. In repose positions you may just see the last tip of the quill only. Some undercutting is still a good idea to emphasize (exaggerate) the strong line of the tail and its feathers. This provides something of a compositional balance with the detail of the head.

THE HEAD

Let's start with the feathers. On most heads these lie flat and are tiny, narrow and spiked. You really have a choice. If one is to go for slightly more realism, this is done by carving tiny, very narrow vees with the open end of the vee towards the beak. By burning the two arms of the vee starting each time at the meeting point, the point is emphasized – this simulates the overlap onto the next feather. The alternative is to simply incise a mass of short lines.

It is important to get the orientation of the head feathers correct – they always lie along the axis from the beak and down to the body. This means that some go straight over the top of the head and

Here the head feathers are spiky and end in a ruff at the back of the neck. They are first deep-gouged with a disc shaped milling cutter.

After milling, the spikes are created with a pointed pyro burner.

The much finer feathers of an early Pintail's head are burnt with a hard metal pyrograph. The line of flow is from the beak down the neck. The eyes are mounted in plastic wood and should have been recessed a little deeper with clearer eyelids.

85

down the neck to the cape. Those starting at the side of the beak cross the cheek and then start to dip down the side of the neck. Others go from under the beak straight down the front of the neck.

Of course, some species have distinctive extra head feathers or plumes. The Plover has an upward curving fine point; the Tufted Duck has a little ponytail-like set of feathers down the back of the skull; the Wood Duck has a long back and sides 'pudding bowl cut' that ends in a distinctive skirt around the back of the neck; while the male Merganser has two pointed spikes straight out to the rear – and there are many others. It is best not to try for too much realism in representing most of these; the nature of wood does not sustain it. Allow for the feature in marking out the blank and then gash the tuft deeply with a fine cutter and finally using a long narrow-pointed burning tool make deep incisions.

Again there are species differences when it comes to the eyes. All birds have eye 'sockets' and eyelids. Some such as hawks and eagles have deeply incised eye sockets with heavy, beetling eyebrows. Once the zone has been appropriately carved and smoothed the eyes are fitted before the tiny lines are burnt in to represent the minute feathers that surround the eyes and the wrinkles of the eyelids.

It was earlier recommended that you drilled the holes for the eyes when you had finished carving the blank. Here opinions differ. Some like to drill at least a pilot hole before shaping the eye sockets and brows; others like to get all the shaping and smoothing done before drilling the actual hole. Sometimes it is not easy to prevent a drill drifting within a shaped socket as the hole is started. What is important is that you do not fit the eye bead itself until you have completely finished shaping and smoothing the whole area. You only have to touch a glass eye with a burr or abrasives and it is

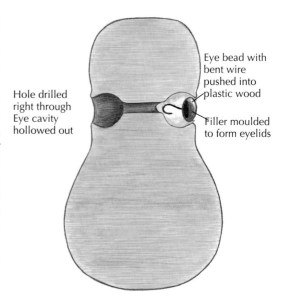

Hole drilled right through Eye cavity hollowed out

Eye bead with bent wire pushed into plastic wood

Filler moulded to form eyelids

The eye socket for bead fixing.

permanently scratched.

I like to insert the eyes into a hollowed chamber – these are undercut using a tiny ball-head burr. The wire of the eye is cut about 1.5cm (⅝in) behind the ball – the wire is then bent back to form a loop. The socket into which it is to be fitted is filled with plastic wood of an appropriate colour and the eye is pushed in until it is at the right depth and a little of the plastic wood has squeezed out round the edges. This is quickly shaped to form eyelids using dental probes. It is then left to set hard to be finally trimmed with a medium-heat pyro point.

You have three options on eyes. First, eyes of the correct size and colour for your species can be bought from either taxidermists or carvers' suppliers, or you can, from the same source, buy a supply of clear eyes and apply a little acrylic paint to their backs to obtain the colour that you require. The third option is for black eyes only. Here you can turn eyes from a piece of Buffalo horn and then polish it to a brilliant black – this traditional approach is only cheaper if you do not cost your time!

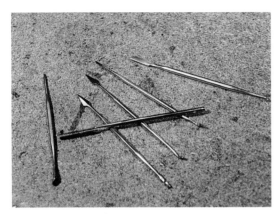

Wax modelling tools used for moulding plastic wood.

Each species of bird has its own very distinctive beak arrangement, even the basic profiles vary enormously within a single type. There is no 'standard' duck's beak – they range from the wide spoon-ended bill of the Shoveller to the distinctly pointed one of the Merganser. Between these extremes are a whole range of rounded and square-ended forms. The varieties are a little less well-defined across the owls and the hawks. Waders and shorebirds have mostly long and thin beaks, and although many are straight, there are well-known exceptions – the Avocet with its distinctive upward-pointed stone turner, and the long downward-curved probe of the Curlew and others.

Beaks are normally carved to shape and then sanded. The burning tool may be used to detail the serrated lamellae on the outer edge of the lower bill, and although many carvers use a long tapered burr to make the nostrils, I like to burn these in. The rest of the beak is carved with gouges and small burrs.

At the front of the duck's beak there is a distinct nose or Pin. This is often coloured differently from the rest of the beak. The pin is sometimes rounded but may have a concave surface. You will need to check reference drawings for the species that you are working on.

The lower bill on ducks closes inside the upper section and usually has three longitudinal grooves on the underside. One starts at the neck and finishes close to the front tip. The other two are close to the outer edge. All this detail is carved with fine burrs, and on pyroed birds looks better if slightly scorched with a broad-tip burner.

If the rest of the bird is in a brown feather-burnt style you may find it looks better if the beak is stained with a wood dye – shaded light or dark according to species.

Remembering what was said earlier about the run of the grain, you may find it inappropriate to carve the beak in one piece with the head. With ducks in standard posture there is no problem; owls and hawks too present no difficulty. It is the long beaks of waders that require special attention. Even if the beak is held straight out along the axis of the body, it is often better if it is carved from a harder wood than the Lime or Jelutong body. If the beak is angled or curved in any way it should be carved separately and inserted.

Ash is a good wood for separate beaks, although I frequently use Oak. Having a small lathe available, I turn the blank with an end dowel of about 3cm long and to an exact 10mm diameter.

Birds that are to have inserted beaks are specially prepared. When the outline is first drawn on the plank a small block is sketched in where the root of the bill will come. This block is then left uncarved until the whole of the rest of the bird is shaped, carved and smoothed. Only at this stage is a deep 10mm hole drilled into the block. The drill is very carefully angled for the set of the beak.

Curved beaks are bent from straight blanks. The method of bending that you are to use will determine your next few steps. If you have access to a bending iron, then shout for joy. I am fortunate in

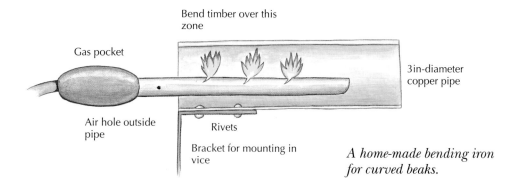

A home-made bending iron for curved beaks.

having an iron for bending the ribs (sides) of guitars. But for my first guitar I used to use a home-made bender.

In its crudest form a bending iron can be a length of 3in (7.5cm) diameter copper pipe with a bracket firmly riveted on. The bracket is then held in a metal vice. A gas poker is run inside the pipe to create the necessary heat. Simple but effective. I have seen similar devices with ceramic electric fire elements mounted in, but this is dangerous when used with wet wood.

The wood (with a 10mm diameter turned or carved end spigot) is soaked for a few hours and is then bent round the hot iron. To avoid burning your fingers use wood blanks that are longer than required and wear a pair of industrial gloves. It also helps if the wood has a flat side which is applied to the wood.

An alternative to this form of bending iron is to use a length of plastic drainpipe; suspend the wood in this and then pass steam through for a few hours. Bending does take time and is a bit messy, but it is worth it. There is NOTHING worse than accidentally hitting or dropping a bird and breaking off a cross-grained beak.

With the blank bent it can be crudely shaped with a spokeshave. A belt sander is also quite useful. The spigot is now cut to length for the pre-drilled hole. PVA glue is applied within the hole and the beak

pushed home and given 24 hours to dry. Finally the front of the head is carved and faired into the beak, and the beak is finally shaped and sanded.

This beautiful Curlew was knocked over when dusting. The beak was not a heat bent one.

— 8 —

SQUATTERS OUT

Not all ducks float on water, and certainly very few birds other than ducks squat – except when sitting on the nest. So the standard posture that we use for our first few duck carvings will soon fail to satisfy our creative urge.

Probably one of your first adventures will be to carve a sleeping duck. Some just 'hunch', they pull the head down into their shoulders and close their eyes. Others turn the head round some 120 degrees, tilt it on its side, and tuck the bill into the scapular feathers. Now you can only see one eye, and that will be closed. A nice variation on this pose is to squat the bird on a half log; the tips of the webbed feet may or may not be seen. At this point you have a choice – do you take a real half log and work the underside of the bird to fit it, or do you carve the whole bird and the log from a single block. It is quite fun to carve a featureless piece of Lime to make it look like a weathered piece of driftwood.

A pair of sleeping Teal – they require beak staining and overall finishing with Danish Oil.

The next variation to the standard pose may well be to have the head turned slightly. If this is to be a duck it can still be cut from a single block as a duck's bill does not need great mechanical strength, and you are probably not going to get to the point where you have got dangerous cross grain. However both for ease of carving and timber economy it is better to carve the head and body from separate pieces. Plan your rough cutting so that the joint between the head and the body comes just where the neck starts to leave the top of the body.

Complete the cutting and shaping of the profiles of the body and the head while they are still separate. The one essential is to have a perfect fit between the two elements. If you have a planer a single sweep along the top of the body is useful. A sanding table can also be used, particularly to flatten off the base of the neck. You can however get a good fit without mechanical aids. Saw and plane the joint as flat as possible then sandwich a piece of 120 grit abrasive paper loose between the two elements and rub them together with a circular motion. After a few turns invert the paper and carry on. When you are satisfied that you have a seamless fit, mark the centres and drill for a 10mm dowel.

You will find that it greatly facilitates much of the shaping of the body if you do not yet glue the two parts together. Without the head in position you have a clean sweep for the draw-knife or spoke-shave. Take care however not to encroach on the flat that you have left for the joint.

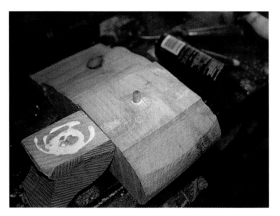

Gluing on a separate head. The grain in the head is angled up along the beak line.

And much later. The line of neck feathers completely hides the joint.

There is not much work that you can do on the loose head unless you are going to do your waste removal with a coarse burr as you have not got anything with which to hold the head to allow knife or gouge carving.

When you are ready, make the joint using a good wood glue and allow it to set. The head and neck can now be shaped and the neck faired into the body. A lot of this work has to be done with small carving tools or burrs.

While at this level of duck carving let's take a quick look at the tradition of hollowing. Here the body is made of two (or more) planks. The head/neck piece is also separate. Cut two short lengths of plank each long enough for the bird's body. Tack the two together with a central blob of hot melt glue. Trace the top view outline on the double plank and band-saw the shape.

If you go in for the idea of taping the offcuts back in position and drawing on and cutting the side profile, then do this, but leave the main area of the top of the back flat except for the small breast curve and the tail zone.

Now open the two halves at the gluing joint and, holding the two halves, sketch on the area you wish to hollow. Unfortun-

ately it is only rarely that you can hollow out with a router. You do not have the area to support the flat base of the router. If you have a bench press, then this is very useful. Most of the waste can be removed with a series of plunges using the largest available diameter of Forstener bit. Preset the required depth, but do not forget when hollowing the top that you must allow for the slope of the shoulders and wings. It was to facilitate hollowing that we kept the top of the back flat.

If you do not have a large Forstener or saw tooth bit make a series of holes with your largest drill, and cut the waste away with chisels. Don't forget when you finally glue the top and bottom halves together to drop in a small pebble or a small steel nut. The tradition dictates that the finished decoy should rattle when shaken.

We have already mentioned one important variation on the standard pose – this is displaying or calling. Here the male bird makes itself look as proud and eye-catching as possible. Birds display in different ways. With some the head is tilted backwards and the beak is opened to call. You can therefore see the tongue which now has to be carved, and the inside of the beak cavity needs to be hollowed. The tail is certainly 'displayed' –

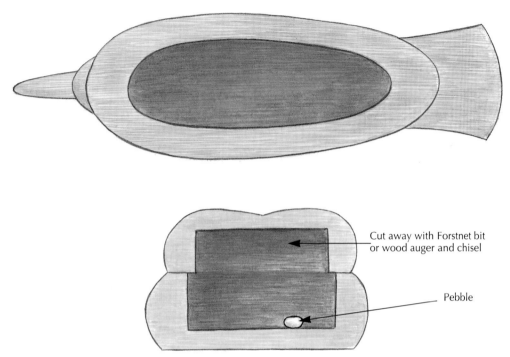

Cut away with Forstnet bit or wood auger and chisel

Pebble

The hollowing zones for a traditional decoy.

cocked up and fanned. Sometimes the wings are, while still semi-folded, held stiffly just proud of the body. Many displaying poses are not difficult, and in a few moments we must consider some of the carving implications.

A carving tradition in working shore birds and waders is to mount them on a block of wood using a single length of wood dowel or metal dowel to act as the legs. Beyond the length to which the wood is cut, there is no attempt at the representation of reality. With birds intended for display a piece of 10mm Ramin dowel will suffice – this is usually dark stained. If on the other hand the bird is to be or even to simulate a working decoy then the dowel is not strong enough and the old tradition was to use an 18in (46cm) length of Bamboo cane – later replaced with metal pipe. This is painted an appropriate colour. The end can now be stuck into the wet sand of the seashore.

With waders and shore birds you can be much more realistic and you would certainly do this if you were producing a feather-detailed and painted bird, if you use built-up legs. From carvers' suppliers you can obtain metal legs for the specific type of bird you are carving. These are made in pewter which is cast around a stiff metal wire core. At the top is a spigot to fit in a hole drilled in the underside of the bird's body. The metal legs have fully detailed feet with a length of the wire core left hanging for insertion into a base block. Once painted these metal legs are so lifelike that they almost look artificial!

You can always make your own metal-based legs and you will come across many different approaches. Which you choose will depend upon your skills and the resources that you have available. A local blacksmith made a nice pair of legs for my

A pair of cast pewter legs for a Godwit.

Grey Heron. He used 'knobbly' reinforcing rods for the main length, built up the knees with weld metal, and welded on scraps of finer reinforcing for the feet. Curlew legs have been made from galvanized fencing wire cores with hand-moulded epoxy putty for the knees and skin. Here lengths of finer wire were wound on for the feet with the putty holding them in place. Unfortunately wire that is strong enough to support the bird is usually of a metal that you can not simply solder; so without a brazing kit or a friendly blacksmith you are limited.

When fitting metal legs – either into the body spigot hole or the feet to the mounting block, use an epoxy resin glue such as Araldite.

Some of the species of birds that are popular with carvers (and the buying public) do not need metal legs. You can also minimize the need by the posture that you choose.

Owls, hawks and eagles have feathered 'gaiters'. Usually when the bird stands there is a very short length of leg that can be seen between the bottom of the gaiter and the top of the foot. You have two options. One is to 'fake it' by extending the gaiter down onto the foot – this provides two thicker supports for the bird. The other is to drill up through the base and on up through the leg into the body. Four-inch (10cm) nails are then pushed up into the Araldite-filled drill holes. If you adopt this latter approach you will find that it is not always easy to get the position of the drill hole absolutely correct up the centre of the leg. If you are unsure you might consider fixing the nails in position before finally carving the leg. If you now accidentally expose a section of the nail you can make up the leg with plastic or resin wood and carve it appropriately.

This owl is a one-piece carving. The gaiters have been taken down to cover the feet and the tail is substantially attached to the carved base.

A superb Woodcock carved and painted by Judith as a Royal Golden Wedding Commission.

A Christmas craft-fair stand at the NEC in the 1980s with some of my first birds.

If you are relying on wooden legs (with or without extended gaiters) then it is strongly recommended that the bird's tail is carved so that it is resting on the base and is therefore integral with the block on which the bird is standing.

So what is the bird going to stand on? If you are using metal legs, then it could be anything. You might take a real log, give it a flat base and then stick the legs into that. You can even take an attractive piece of rockery stone, drill holes in it with a masonry drill and glue the legs into it.

If, on the other hand, you have chosen the wooden-legs route then the base and the bird has to be carved from one solid block. You now have to work the base in some way. Most carvers carve the base. The simplest, but still very effective, idea is to carve it so that it looks like a piece of weathered wood. Much more ambitious is to carve some naturalistic element of the bird's habitat. The bird might be sitting in a carved nest. Humming-birds can be shown with their beaks probing into a carved lily head. Owls are often shown with a mouse under a claw; Ospreys standing on their supper – a carved trout on a piece of rocky river bank; Eagles on a rabbit, and so on.

If you do embark upon carvings of this complexity you will probably wish to keep the finished piece for yourself, or give it to a loved one. If you do sell it must be for many hundreds of pounds. You do your own self-esteem, your reputation as a carver, and the whole woodworking and carving profession no good at all if you do not demand a fair price. Charging anything less than the National Minimum Wage hourly rate for your efforts downgrades all of us in the eyes of the public! Of course you should be charging much more and the best decoy carvers get many times that rate – so might you one day! Some of the pyrographed birds in this book have sold for over £500.

There are less than a dozen major craft fairs across the country which attract the sort of buying public that will purchase carved birds at the price that you must charge, and the normal outlet is through selected galleries.

We now have birds in sitting or standing poses, wings folded and tails down. We rather jumped ahead of ourselves just now by talking about beautiful carved 'scenic' bases. The third stage of our development as carvers is likely to be a little more mundane.

The next venture for many carvers is pieces with raised wings. Birds raise their wings for a number of different reasons. First they may be stretching or preening. Perching birds will occasionally raise both wings to a vertical position. First they go to full stretch. They sometimes follow this with a shaking – a sort of shimmying motion and even, occasionally, with a couple of slow flaps. The wings are then drawn down and are now gently shaken as they fold in. Preening often follows.

In preening, the bird will work on one wing at a time – the other remains folded, although usually not tucked into the pocket. Preening is the action of drawing each feather in turn through the half-open beak. Obviously the head is twisted round, the feathers are opened, and the one being worked upon is likely to be arched under the tension. If preening postures are of interest to you, then you will need to sally forth with a camera – illustrations are rare, and I know of no available ready-drawn plans. Your searches may be more productive.

Hawks and Eagles do something that other species do not. When they have made a kill, they will 'hood' their prey while feeding to hide it from other predators. Hooding is the process of stretching the wings out sideways with the outer wing section turned down. The feathers are fully extended as in flight.

Two views of a stuffed Buzzard to be turned into a carving plan.

The first step. The pictures have been line scanned into a computer. The image is then enlarged to life size on a photocopier (see also page 22).

One of the most spectacular carvings that you could ever imagine is an eagle hooding a rabbit carcass. The best place to look for hooding postures is on TV; you will often see Vultures and Eagles hooding in the wildlife programmes. Try taking a reference photo of the TV screen (use 1/30th second shutter speed).

The next category of natural wings-out postures are where the birds are about to launch into the air, or are just touching down on landing. Field observation will soon lead you to identify that there are distinct differences between the wing sets of birds that are taking off from when they are landing. In the latter there is a strong element of 'flaps down' – the wings are held at a braking angle to the line of flight, and the secondaries are definitely tipped down. In making carvings of this style you frequently have to rely on artificial aids or in faking some element. It may, for instance, be necessary to have the feet and tail just touching some part of the base, and you will have mechanical problems with the strength of some feathers – more of this in a few moments.

The support problem becomes even greater when carving birds in flight. Do you have it skimming and just touching a metal reinforced wave tip? Do you have it on a clearly visible metal rod above an abstract base? Does it hang on a wire from the ceiling? or what? Obviously you will have to use one of these (or similar) devices – all are employed and very acceptable – so, again, the choice is yours. A very effective arrangement is to have a board that can be hung on the wall. The birds are then fixed to this with horizontal metal rods.

It is all very well talking about all the

many different styles and postures that we can portray, but what about the carving processes? Everything you have to do, however complicated the piece, has already been discussed or at least touched upon earlier in this book. The issues of positioning the plan on the plank, and the processes of shaping, cutting and burning the wood are the same whatever the posture. The problems that we now need to look at a little more deeply have also already been mentioned; they can be summarized in two phrases – gaining cutting access, and mechanical strength. In fact there is a considerable inter-relationship between the two problems, and there is often a single, common solution.

There are times when the detail that you want to carve is in such a position that it is masked by another element of the carving. It is difficult to get in even with a flexible shaft-driven carving tool, and impossible to access with a burner. The answer is often to make the blank in pieces, which are worked separately and finally joined and finished together.

You often have to adopt exactly the same solution to deal with mechanical problems. A few moments ago we talked about legs which were made of a stronger (metal) material, or that were reinforced with a hidden metal rod (a 4in (10cm) nail). In the last chapter we looked at beaks (particularly curved ones) that would have no mechanical strength if carved in wood that was in the least degree cross-grained. The solution there was to make the beak separately in straight-grained timber, and then to heat or steam-bend it, and to then insert and glue it into a pre-drilled hole.

The more complex the carving, and the further you get away from the standard pose, the more frequently you will have to use inserts. Many carvers use inserts for the primary and secondary feathers on simple squatting ducks. The little curled feather above the tail of a male mallard has to be cut from sheet metal or a few laminates of thin ply.

Inserts are elements of the carving – possibly a group or even a single feather that are cut from separate pieces of timber and are then inserted into slots let into the main body of the carving. Obviously the inserts are always cut along the grain to give maximum mechanical strength.

A perching Kestrel being prepared for wing inserts.

Wingtip inserts are not difficult although you will find them a little tricky until you have done a few. You first shape and profile the overlying feather group, undercutting the edge. Next, working first with a drill and then a miniature morticizing bit, you cut a slot under the overlying feathers. Your insert will be glued into this slot.

Three glues feature amongst those most widely used. For fixing metal inserts there is nothing to beat epoxy resin glues – Araldite, already mentioned, being a great favourite. For fixing small wooden inserts (and securing small splits) many favour the Superglues. Larger joints, laminating, fixing feather inserts, dowelling, attaching heads and so on, always cause me to reach for the PVA wood glues. Lest there be misunderstanding, for furniture-making I still require the 'give' in traditional Pearl glues, or in pieces not subject to loading and movement I might choose the stronger Cascemite.

There are a number of approaches to the making of actual inserts. The first and simplest to carve but most difficult to fit, is the carving from a single piece of solid wood. Here you cut the outline and then carve the butt until it fits snugly into the slot that you have already carved on the

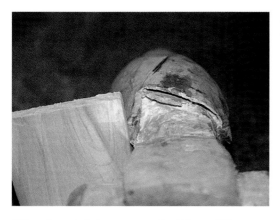

Wing insert slots are carved with a milling cutter.

bird's body. Once this is a good fit you can then carve and burn on the feathers before gluing the insert into the bird. Some carvers prefer, however, to shape, fit, and glue the insert in before finally carving and burning it.

The second and third methods are to build up the insert piece by piece, cutting each feather separately. In one you use thin slices of the wood from which the body is made; the other uses 1mm ply. This or similar imperial grade, is available in some of the better model shops where it is sold for building flying models; it makes very thin, extremely strong feathers! The leaves of the wing or tail-feather groups are built up and glued

The body is feather-burnt before the fragile inserts are fitted. Feather breaks have yet to be burnt in.

The full depths of the slots can be seen.

The inserts have been pushed into place.

together before the whole insert is slotted into the body. Using the build-up approach does require that you finely adjust the shape and depth of the slot to match the insert that you have now constructed – it is easier to adjust the shape of the insert than it is to modify the slot.

Obviously the whole purpose of inserts is to be able to carve the piece with the grain lying down its axis where the axis is distinctly different from the lie of the grain in the main body.

Tails are most frequently carved integral with the body. Inserts are used only when the tail is cocked or is to be very thin in section.

The biggest inserts of all are where the whole or a substantial part of the wing requires a different grain orientation to the wood of the body. This means that almost every conceivable flying posture will involve wing inserts.

It is tempting to make the whole or at least the main part of the wing or wings from a single piece with a squared block at the butt; this can then be slotted into a neat square recess in the body. If the wings are spread in a full flight position this presents no problem as you will probably use a single plank to produce the

99

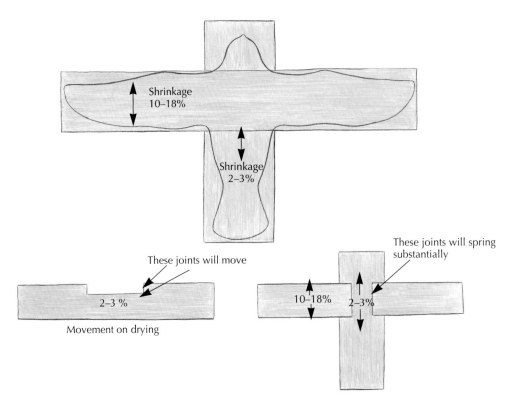

Shrinkage
10–18%

Shrinkage
2–3%

These joints will spring
substantially

These joints will move

2–3 %

Movement on drying

10–18%   2–3%

The shrinkage problem with wing blocks.

The power of movement in wood. In the Italian marble quarries Romans gouged channels into which were driven dry wood wedges. The wedges were then soaked and as they expanded they sheared huge blocks away from the bedrock.

100

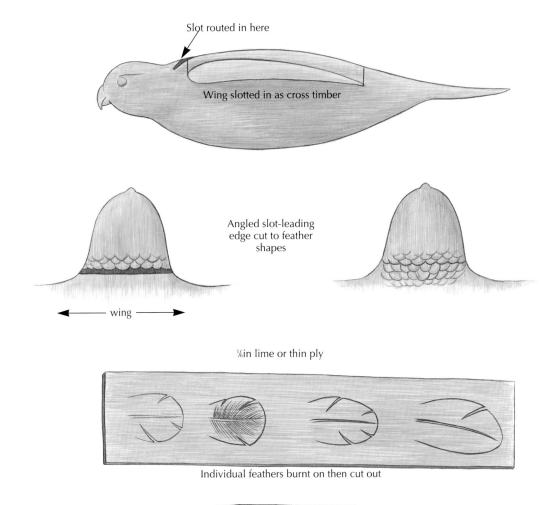

Slot routed in here

Wing slotted in as cross timber

Angled slot-leading
edge cut to feather
shapes

← wing →

⅛in lime or thin ply

Individual feathers burnt on then cut out

Each feather relieved at edge. Sides burnt.
Fine wedge taper on front edge

Scapular inserts to hide a wing joint that might give.

complete wings. If, however the wings are raised or angled upwards you will almost certainly have the two wings cut separately. Again you may consider a simple squared block at the root of each wing sitting in squared recesses either side of the top of the body. The blocks may even join as shoulders in the centre of the back. You will of course improve the strength of such a joint by dowelling. Unfortunately this apparently simple solution is asking for trouble – it is not just a question of the mechanical strength of the joint.

Let's go back to what we were saying about the movement of wood on drying. A block of wood or a plank or whatever will shrink three or four times as much across its width (across the grain) as it will along its length (along the grain). Even if you start with properly dried wood the natural rise and fall of the moisture content due to humidity and absorption is likely to cause a similar differential in the movement. This means that in time a crack or gap will appear around the joint, in fact the glue joint may eventually give totally. Hence the need for dowelling as well as 'flexible' glue. It is essential therefore that to hide the unsightly crack, the block is inserted under an overlapping feather group, or that the joint of the block to the body is itself masked under a small secondary insert. In the case of straight across wings the fitting of a slotted-in covering insert is not difficult. If the wings are angled into the body the making and fitting of an insert of scapular feathers across the angled joint is a nightmare.

Just to reinforce this message, here is a small deviation. Two and more thousand years ago, the Romans in marble and earlier the Egyptians in granite punched a row of shallow holes (of about 6–8in (15–20cm) deep) or made a long groove into the bedrock in their quarries, they plugged the holes with tight fitting dry wooden wedges and then poured water onto the wood. As the pegs absorbed moisture they expanded and eventually the whole block (possibly 4–10ft (1.2–3m) thick) split away from the bed. Using only such methods single 100ft (30m) blocks were produced for the carving of monoliths such as 'Cleopatra's Needle'. Such is the movement and power of expanding and contracting wood.

A joint between two blocks of wood, each moving to different extents and in different directions as the humidity changes, will be subject to just as much force as was produced to split the stone in the days before the invention of Black Powder or Gelignite.

My ultimate carving – which to this day I have never found the time to start – is to be a Buzzard with wings hooded or raised to full upwards stretch. The fleshy part of the wings will be inserted as blocks but covering the joint area will be a whole series of small scapular inserts (each feather separate). But then the real fun starts. Each of the primaries and most of the secondaries will themselves be separate inserts. Each feather is to be made of a separate piece of thin, heat-bent timber. The finished work should be divine – in more senses than one!

THE END OR THE BEGINNING?

How will you finish what you have started?

In front of you will be a bird in one of four basic styles. It may be smooth carved in beautifully figured wood with or without a few suggestions of feather outlines to the wings or tail; it may be that the feather-burnt stage that you have now reached is to be the finished state; or you could now be going on to painting. If it is to be painted your final goal could still be in one of two forms. For the first of these, the Slick form, the bird will now be looking very similar to that of our first category – smooth and with little or no detail. In this case the carving may have been made up of indifferent wood, possibly even built up from several planks or pieces. The second pre-painting condition – for a realistic bird – will have some form of incised feather detail that may have been burnt, tool gouged, or both.

Each style now needs appropriate treatment and finishing. In all cases there is likely to be some cleaning up to do.

Let's look first at the smoothing off that we have to do for either natural wood finish or flat painting. First, any detail has

Decision point – should this two-piece blank be sanded smooth for painting as a slick, or have a little more detail carved in for feather burning?

to be smoothed. If any relief carving of the wing feathers has been done the edges have to be carefully cleaned up. There is nothing worse than seeing unevenness or fluffy surfaces along feather-edges. At this stage high-speed burrs are not appropriate. A small selection of riffler files will allow you to get into awkward corners. You can also wrap small pieces of very fine grit abrasive paper round the files to finish off. It is time-consuming but essential. Take particular care when working around the eyes to avoid scratching the glass. With the detail cleaned there are now the main areas.

It is when you reach this stage for the first time that you begin to realize the importance of carving very clean, smooth steps around the profiles of feathers. Often when you try to finish these with burrs you create tiny ridges and valleys within the steps. If you now paint or polish it you will get a terrible shock! It will look like the Scottish Highlands. A metal shaded desk lamp is useful. Position it so that it shines across the surface and reduce all other ambient light. Move the bird around in the beam and look for shadows. Mark each. Let's hope that you have not created hours of riffler file work for yourself, and that you do not have too much cleaning up to do before you have a carving that looks beautifully smooth and totally free of any bumps or hollows.

Rotary sanding devices can be used but they are limited in their efficacy when dealing with complex rounded shapes. They must be run slowly with 360 grit being the coarsest grade of abrasive used, and 400 being preferred. Other than for working in a step corner or a steep radiused concave area, drum discs make more marks than they remove.

Some of the new multi-motion orbital detail sanders with a very fine abrasive paper on a cushion mount are absolutely marvellous. Obviously, however, they can not get right into all corners. So in the end it comes down to abrasive papers. I have a strong preference for good quality wet or dry in 240, 320 and 400 grit. The grit bonding seems more reliable on wet or dry and certainly lasts longer than most ordinary sandpapers. Wherever possible sand only along the grain, although an orbital motion is fine at 400 grit.

Riffler files for cleaning edges around feathers and wings.

If the bird is now to be smooth painted then it can be laid to one side.

Natural wood birds need to be quite as smooth and blemish free as those for painting, so the treatment thus far is the same.

Now you have some choices. First the completely natural wood, if left untreated, looks dead and lifeless and will certainly have a drab colour. It will also quickly mark and attract dust. The wood needs to be oiled or polished, and you may even wish to consider staining. Before you do anything else, decide on the colour for the beak (and the leg/s). These you will probably stain with wood dye or stain. I find that Jacobean, Dark, or Medium Oaks or Walnut are my most frequent choices.

A little oiling will bring out the natural colour and enhance the grain or figure of the whole bird. Oil will also penetrate the surface where it will dry to an invisible skin. Teak Oil is good, but I prefer Danish Oil. Linseed Oil is inclined to leave an oily film. Applying more than one coat of any oil increases the surface film and can eventually give a slight glossiness. Aged, or partially oxidized Danish Oil is particularly prone to give a varnish-like finish (if that is what you require). Once the oil has dried, smooth birds can be given a polish – ideally with a beeswax-based wood polish.

The next set of possibilities are the various stain and wax concoctions that are now on the market. These can impart a slight staining as well as a surface gloss. While these are extremely quick and easy and are ideal for some applications they do not give the depth of sheen that you require for a carving.

Various traditional furniture-making approaches may be considered. There are the dark browns and blacks that can be produced in some woods by fuming. A range of lighter browns can be achieved by chemical staining or, in the completely opposite direction, there are liming and bleaches than can take the colour away.

Woods with a high tannin content, such as Oak, and to a lesser extent Chestnut respond well to 'Fuming'. This means enclosing the piece in an airtight chamber into which is introduced 880 strength ammonia. The fumes react with the tannins to cause a deep blackish brown 'stain'.

A similar effect can be created with any wood by first soaking the piece in an iron-rich solution – gardeners' Moss Killer is ideal! Again the soaked piece is fumed.

For a bird carver the airtight container can be a strong polythene bag. Extreme caution has to be exercised in handling ammonia of this strength. A deep breath can choke you to death, so the process is done outside on a breezy day with you standing upwind of the ammonia bottle. With the bird and a bowl of liquid in the bag the mouth is sealed and left for a few days.

Wood dyes can be used in one of two ways. One is to simply colour the wood to any colour of your choice, and the other is to use more lifelike colours for the different parts of the bird.

Recently I have seen natural wood-carved birds which have been give subtle treatment with wood dyes. Here the colours were mixed and used almost as water colours – so it is almost a painting process with lighter highlights and darker shadows and subtle shades. The birds were then oiled and polished and looked 'antiqued' and very effective.

One completely non-representational approach can also be very effective. Some timbers such as Ash have a markedly different texture between the summer and winter growth rings. The carved bird is washed with a single main body colour and allowed to dry. A little gold acrylic paint is now rubbed over the whole piece in a soft cloth. This leaves traces of the gold in the more grainy rings of the wood and the main body is rubbed clear. Again

This Curlew body in Elm was soaked in Moss Killer (to introduce Iron) and then fumed with strong (880) ammonia.

this can be both subtle and beautiful. The skill is in the choice of the colour.

There is much less preparatory work to do in cleaning up the birds for feather burning, but you may need to do some fine tuning. What makes the birds so attractive is that each feather barb is incised and the groove is lined with burnt wood (charcoal). If you do nothing to it and leave it like that, in time and with normal household dusting, the charcoal will rub away. You will still see the feather detailing but it will be less well defined and nowhere near as dramatic.

If the feather burning is merely a precursor to realistic painting, then you are better off without the loose charcoal. To get rid of it brush over the entire surface with an old toothbrush or a fine brass bristled suede brush. Again no further work is required and the bird can be put by for painting. We will start to look

at painting techniques in the next chapter.

You may wish to brush some of the feathers even if not going on to painting. When we were looking at the burning process, mention was made of the breasts of Owls where we used the very lightest of touches with the pyro. You can effectively differentiate light and dark areas of the bird's natural colour by brushing the charcoal in some areas and not in others. Here the brass suede brush is the best tool.

Many of my birds are not brushed at all. I like the rich darkness of the burnt lines. Two coats of Danish Oil will actually 'fix' any loose charcoal in the scorch lines. And so the feather-burnt bird is now finished.

Once you have moved on from standard-pose squatting birds you will be faced by the question of bases. Earlier we considered one-piece carvings where the bird was mounted on a carved base. At

The finished feather-burnt Kestrel has an integral base carved to represent a post top.

that time the possibility of 'scenic' bases was raised, but it was also suggested that the base might be carved to suggest a piece of weathered wood.

Obviously there are a number of possibilities. I have two favourites. Small squatting ducks are carved integral with the base block that is itself fashioned to look like a half log. The top is then textured to look like the bark of the log and the two end half moons are cut and burnt to give an impression of annular rings.

The second, more appropriate to standing hawks and owls, has a block carved to simulate the top of an old, weathered post with radial check marks and splits down the face.

Any texturing is done with a narrow gouge and the hollows are then charred with a broad pyrograph tip. Deep splits are cut with a medium vee, deepened with a micro vee and then burnt with the tip of the pyrograph.

There is clearly much more scope when the base can be separated from the bird – as when metal, or single stick legs are to be

A bird in the master class. Judith Nicoll's Jack Snipe taking off from a branch.

107

used. Here you are pushed in two distinct directions. The first is to abandon all impressionistic attempts at realism and to use a shaped (round, square, oval and so on) block of wood. This may be painted, or left natural and polished. The alternative is to use a real piece of wood – a half log (with the bark on), a branch or twig; or to build up a platform of natural materials.

You will see blocks with sand or sandpaper stuck on with adhesive, and the wader's dowel fixed into that; or you can go the whole Natural History Museum hog and make a small tray with real sand and a painted egg – and so on.

It has to be said that a little 'presentation' can often take a relatively ordinary carving into the master class in the public's eye. Think of the bird in its natural habitat and consider what elements of that environment you could actually use or simulate for the base. Then ask yourself 'How can I best set the bird off? How would I like to see it in my own home?' With a nice 'cuddly' standard posture duck everybody will want to stroke it – so the best means of presentation can sometimes be simply a little printed card saying 'Please stroke me'!

— 10 —

TOOLS OF THE TRADE

Wherever you put this chapter, it will be wrong. It could have been placed right at the beginning – some think it best to think about and buy all their tools before they go out and look for birds to carve. Others find a bird, get all excited about it and then go on hold while the tool-kit is built up. Of course we could all whittle a bird or two before we really tool up. Probably most of us just blunder on. We start with the ordinary household DIY tools that we have; then we see things in catalogues and think 'Oh that looks interesting!' We finish up with some really useful items, but also an awful lot of gimmicks that just collect dust on the shelf. Most of us learn from our mistakes and eventually build a kit with which we are reasonably satisfied. Personally I like to have tried out a few things and learnt what to look for before really kitting out. You make fewer mistakes that way. So the chapter could come in the middle, or even be placed at the end as an appendix reference.

One thing you quickly learn is not to cost up what you have spent! If the chapter on tools had been positioned right at the beginning of the book, you might well have blanched at the possible expense and decided that carving was not for you. Certainly, few carvers dare to cost up the value of the tool-kit that they eventually arrive at. However, it need not be that way – bird carving can be one of the least expensive areas of woodworking. At least that is what they all tell me!

As we said right at the beginning you may be able to achieve all that you want and to develop a style of your own using nothing more than a whittling knife. Equally fortunate are those who have come to bird carving having already been involved in woodworking and who have a superbly equipped workshop with most of the hand and power tools that they will ever need. Now their additional requirements are just the odd one or two special gouges, a number of burrs and a few carver's peculiars.

So the choice of eventually including this chapter here was deliberate. You now know what the various stages in the process involve, which enables you to consider the tools that you need in context. You will also by now have some idea of the style/s that you wish to pursue. So this chapter is part summary, and also part recommendation. It will naturally be very biased as it will be *my choice* of tool – not only in terms of type, but even make and size. I know that some of my carving colleagues have very different ideas; but I also know that some of them envy me for some of the items that I do have.

So for some this may be a chapter to read right through and take action on; for others it will be a mere broad reinforcement of what they already know; and for some a frequent source of dip-in information.

We have seen how different styles of carving require different tooling. What tools you already possess may have prompted you to opt for particular styles.

My start in duck carving came after a decade and a half of deep involvement with heavy, 'artistic' woodturning with a well-equipped workshop that had been built up over that period. My workshop measures 22ft × 12ft (6.5m × 3.5m), but you can house all you need to do bird carving in a 6ft × 6ft (2m × 2m) garden shed.

As a regular writer of magazine articles on woodworking topics I had been sent many new tools to test and review. Some I was given, and some I was delighted to send back. One absolutely lethal power carver I was actually able to get the company to withdraw from the market. This now means that although my workshop equipment could (always) be improved, there is not much that I actually need; and, more importantly, I have had the opportunity of trying out every item that is listed or mentioned.

One thing I learnt a long time ago, you can not compromise on quality. Bowl turners do a lot of power sanding. The actual loading on a ¼in electric drill is not great, but the dust is devastating. Ordinary DIY-quality Black and Decker drills used to last me from 11–12 months; Bosch slightly less. My ½in Black and Decker Professional model is now in its fourteenth year – and it has not even had a service. The record with chain-saws is very similar.

The quality difference between makers is also significant. Cheap edge tools, whether imported or home-produced, are basically useless. Beyond these there are noticeable differences between the tools of some of the better known manufacturers. There are two of the most famous name British manufacturers whose edge tools I will not touch at any price (and they are definitely not the cheapest). I find that Marples standard chisels are surprisingly good, and the old set of their carvers that I use are excellent. Although I made extensive use of the superb Sorby High-Speed Steel turning tools, I have not tried their carvers. Recently, attracted by both the look of the steel and the extremely low price I bought

a small set of carvers sold under the name of Crown (a Sheffield company) and these are serving me extremely well. However, I have to say that at the end of the day I find that the Ashley Isles carvers (and turning tools) are the absolute tops. I have not felt it necessary to try the Japanese chisels that cost hundreds of pounds each!

Interestingly, although I have never needed the service, Ashley Isles offer a lifetime's guarantee on all tools that they sell and also provide a free resharpening service for the life of the tool. What is more they will make tools to order, produce blades with rounded tangs to fit the Bourdet, and even test and re-temper suspect blade of other makes. Refreshingly, their focus upon quality and customer satisfaction far exceeds their concern with profit.

Obviously you need to have tools of a size that is appropriate to the job – but it is not quite as simple as that. The larger the tool (of a given quality) the more it will withstand abuse and the longer it will last. So for rough work go big! When you get into fine detail then you need to have much smaller tools. However, the smaller the edge the more frequently it will require resharpening during a working session.

Let's now consider the various stages of carving and identify the types of tools that might be required. We will also note some of the budget alternatives.

LOGGING

Woodworkers sometimes get offered trees. For the amount of timber that you are likely to need as a bird carver it is best to turn the offer down. You really need prepared blocks or the occasional plank. Logs can be planked on site (where felled) using a Chain Mill (a device with a huge double-headed chain-saw running on rails), or by getting a contractor with a Forestall or similar portable planker (cost of a day's hire – several hundred pounds). The timber then needs kilning or several years of air drying. You need a huge throughput to justify building a kiln. Trying to plank the tree into pieces suitable for drying for your type of carving using an ordinary chain-saw just does not work. So forget those offers of trees!

CUTTING UP THE PLANK

Forget circular saws – unless you can borrow occasional access to a large industrial unit. Anything that you can buy and house in your workshop will not be tough enough for sawing planks of the thickness that we are interested in.

A generally useful tool is a chain-saw, and if you have one you can always try some 'chunky' carving! But, unless you are also going to use it to feed your open fire or stove, I would forget the petrol-driven models and go for an electric drive. There are two heavy-duty electric machines on the market, but they are scarce and expensive. The larger electric DIY units with an 18in (46cm) bar ('bar' = operational blade length) are OK but their fine chain *must* be sharpened each time you use it, so you will need chain-saw files or a Martek (or similar) unit to work off an electric drill. These latter are very effective for light use.

Ideally, to cut out the profiles, you need a large band-saw with something like a 9in (23cm)-plus gape, and a 12in (30cm)-plus deep throat. Small table-top DIY band-saws are too small. The only wearisome alternatives are first good-quality hand-saws with ripping and cross-cut teeth to cut the block, followed by an 18in (46cm) bow-saw to cut the bird's outline.

SHAPING THE BLANK

Do as much of this as you can by edge-tool cutting, reserving the powered burrs for the difficult corners. First, cutting is more aesthetically satisfying; and secondly, burrs cover everything in the workshop with dust. Even with a mask on some dust will also get into your lungs.

Draw-knives take a little more skill than does a spokeshave. They are however much more efficient and certainly more satisfying once you have practised. You can easily control the depth of each cut and you can access quite difficult corners and curves. Two sizes are useful. The main waste remover will have a blade length of 8–12in (20–30cm), then a 4–6in (10–15cm) blade will better access masked recesses. I like the traditional knives (often available on antique stalls for a few pounds), but I have recently acquired a Flexcut KN16 draw-knife. At first sight this does not look tough enough. The blade is a thin, flat piece of steel that looks a bit like those cheap hand tools on market stalls. It can, however, be sharpened to a long-lasting razor edge, but look out for your fingers! Spokeshaves with their finely controlled depth of cut can smooth off more open runs, but both the spokeshaves with the flat and the round soles are becoming increasingly redundant as skill with the knives increases.

Not all the blank can be shaped with a knife. Sometimes there is a substantial amount of waste to be cut away where knife access is not possible. There are two possibilities for dealing with this. The two carpenter's chisels I use are 1in (2.5cm) and 1½in (4cm)-bladed single bevels. They are driven with a round-head mallet or a plastic-headed hammer. The second, and frequently used method is to cut away as much of the waste as can be accessed with a saw – this happens particularly under the primary feathers at the tail, and sometimes around the beak. Three saws may be employed. Big work is done with a standard tennon saw, the corners are then reached with an ordinary modeller's coping saw, and fine detail with small, model-making bladed saws.

DETAIL SHAPING

As will have already emerged from the earlier text, there are two subsets to this section. One we could call the traditional approach using cutting tools – knives, chisels and gouges; and the second, the modern approach using powered grinders and burrs. They could be seen as separate, parallel or duplicate approaches in that either could exist and operate satisfactorily without the other. Most of us do not make the distinction and move back and forth between them both, although there are a few diehard backwoodsmen who will not have a power tool on the place.

There is, of course, the added complication that with the advent of power carvers we now use modern methods of driving edge tools.

We need to look at the two separately.

EDGE TOOL CARVING

From my turning days, I know that High-Speed Steel lasts longer and is good for sharpening on high-speed grinders (It does not blue if 'overdone'). They hold their edge well for periods of heavy use; but, and this is of vital interest to the carver, HSS does not sharpen to as keen an edge as does the old carbon steel (provided that it is of high quality). Hence HSS and similar alloys are no good for carving tools. So the type of steel and the tempering is of critical importance to the carver. Some of the old tools were made of excellent steel – which can not always be

Using a large carpentry chisel for removing waste.

said of some of today's offerings.

You can do a lot worse than to start with a boxed set of carving tools. Ashley Isles's Canterbury set contains twelve tools that meet most basic needs. As a bird carver you will have less use for straight gouges although a couple of, say, 6 and 9mm will be useful (as well as your 25 and 37mm roughers mentioned above).

Curved spoon chisels feature strongly (again 6 and 9mm), as do straight and curved gouges with medium to shallow Us – possibly up to 12 or 15mm in size. There are times when I call upon a spoon gouge front bent and a dog-leg chisel – both at about 9mm. One or two Vee tools are essential.

Most of my edge tools have conventional long handles, but I do find the American style palm-held handles very

Large bent gouge hollowing out the underwing area.

number of tool clips that you need on your board. Most of us end up with at least three times the number of tools than we ever need or use. Five years ago I bought from a local craftsman, who is even more antique than I, a box full of beautiful carvers. They had previously had very little use and since coming into my workshop, *absolutely none!*

Of course, with edge tools you will also need a means of sharpening them. We will be looking at that in the next chapter.

Before leaving edge tools we need to look back briefly at the modern idea of power carving with motor-driven gouges and chisel. In America there are a number of light-weight units available, but of course they are all on 110 volts so you would need a transformer. The Ryobi unit is popular over there. We now have the 240-volt Bosch in the UK. All of these small units have their own special purpose-made cutters offering a very limited range of the basic chisel and gouge profiles.

As has been mentioned when the issue of power carving was raised there are also heavy-duty power chisels. One has been available for some years in the UK, and this is the Bourdet tool made in France and designed for stone sculpture. A very full range of excellent Bourdet wood-carving blades is available, but for my kit I buy unhandled blades from Ashley Isles and grind their tapered square section tangs down to the round to fit the Bourdet handpiece (you do not need a precise round fit). Already more than convinced by Isles quality, this is for me a much cheaper route than buying Bourdet. (*See* the picture on page 58)

Today my conclusion on power gouges is 'Why bother?', certainly as far as bird carving goes. The Bourdet outfit is wonderful for large wood sculptures where it does save time and effort, and is, in fact, more controllable than is a mallet. But it really is not for birds!

useful when working on detail. As was mentioned in Chapter 7, Isles have recently introduced a range of real miniatures with palm handles. There is a scimitar-shaped blade carver to a Ray Gonzales' design. There are then the two tools that I use most of all – both are tiny Vee gouges, one front bent and the other back bent.

Just a word of warning! Carving tools are highly addictive, particularly the antique ones many of which are of the most wonderful steel. Once you become interested in carving you will find it all too easy to justify the purchase of yet another carving tool. You will already possess all that you ever need when you see a superb collection that a retiree is disposing of, and overnight you have doubled the

GRINDING

Power grinders have raised their dusty heads at least three times in our carving processes. The first was during the rough shaping stage where our interest was in rapid removal of waste; the second was in detail carving; and the third was in speeding up the smoothing and sanding processes. The first of these requires substantially different equipment from the other two.

Major shaping requires heavy-duty coarse-grit cutters, and these require powerful motors to drive them. The cutters also operate at high speeds – way above what can be achieved with an electric drill. You also have to be able to approach the bird from all angles and this means that a flexible drive shaft is essential.

There are two suitable units that are generally available on the market – the Pfingst and the Foredom. The Foredom is slightly more expensive, is widely used and is certainly my favourite. There are different sizes of motor and if you plan to make extensive (continuous) use of the tool for a period of time then the top ¼hp unit is recommended. I have the model H.

There are various handpieces for the Foredom and most have collet heads, but one has a small Jacobs chuck. Obviously the adjustable chuck is more versatile, but it is also slightly bulkier so I have the No. 44 collet head unit, and a boxed set of collets covering bit diameters up to ¼in. I rarely use any of the smaller size collets although I have bits that will fit.

My roughing bits are Kutzalls. They include three large coarse cutters (¼in shafts) and three smaller medium cutters of various profiles. I could do with an even bigger variety as they all get a good deal of use, but at between £10 and £15 a piece, there are limits.

The Foredom is sometimes used for one other task. A ¼in shaft, 2in diameter Velcro-faced sanding disc is useful for smoothing a blank intended for a natural wood finished bird. However, there are two precautions. First, the shaft of the disc must be pushed as far into the collet as possible. The discs are not balanced to turn at the speeds possible with a Foredom; the shaft can bend and the discs can fly off the Velcro. The second precaution must now be evident. The foot

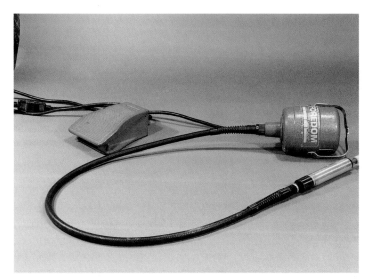

The Foredom model H used for power carving, with the foot-operated 'accelerator' pedal.

The small Minicraft driver after many years of hard work. There is a speed control and a trip button if the motor gets too hot (which it often does!).

control on the unit must be operated very gingerly so that the speed is kept right down. If you are heavy-footed don't even try it!

Obviously the Foredom is not really suitable for detail carving. For fine work you can still use a small flexible drive such as those available for the Dremmel and the Minicraft, but the motive units are now sufficiently small to be operated comfortably and accurately when directly hand-held.

There are two in my workshop and they are extremely useful; both are excellent and either one would suffice. One is the more recent Dremmel that operates direct from the mains, but with a slide step switch on the body it is a little more difficult to adjust; the other is the 12-volt Minicraft which operates through a transformer with an infinitely variable speed controller. My Minicraft has now given me 16 years of fairly heavy use. The Dremmel also has a collet head whereas the Minicraft has a more versatile miniature Jacobs chuck. What is of vital importance is that both have ball-race

heads – a simple bush bearing would not last, as the sideways thrust of grinding can often be considerable. Again this is a bit of quality that is certainly worth paying for.

There are a number of different types of cutter available and you will be interested in most of them.

First there are the smaller shaft sizes of the finer grits of Kutzall. These are always needed to finish shaping and to start smoothing after the coarse Kutzall grind.

The immediate follow-on from the fine Kutzalls are grinders of similar profile, but usually of slightly smaller size where the abrasive is a fine sintered grit of ruby, and then smaller still with fine diamond dust. These are really for smoothing off and finishing detail work. I would almost suggest that you can not have too many different sizes and shapes of burrs. So that gives your family a Christmas present buying list for the next few years.

A few milling cutters are useful for getting deep inside as when carving inside the mouth of calling birds and in hollowing out eye sockets.

The cutting of feather impressions for

Carving and detailing tools.
1) Very fine milling and diamond
cutters.

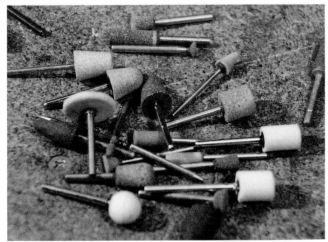

2) Stones used for burnishing.

3) Small sanding drums for
shaping hollows.

painting and the deep grooving to simulate head tuft feathers and similar can be achieved with two types of cutter – one is a flat disc head and the other a fine diamond-shaped profile.

Where there is an option, the extra that you have to pay for solid tungsten carbide cutters is well worth while. It is very easy to overheat plain steel cutters. They easily lose their temper and consequently blunt quickly.

At one of the woodworking shows Proops had a stand. They always have a number of useful bits – the dental probes used in working plastic wood around eye sockets came from there as did magnifiers, drills, milling cutters and others. At one show they had packs of 12 tiny diamond burrs. One, a 10mm long $\times$ 1mm diameter tapered cutter, will deep undercut feathers magnificently. It is also strong enough to withstand the loading of being pulled up through the overhang to make naturally shaped feather breaks. This little kit has been one of my best ever impulse buys.

The marvellous set of carvers bought some time ago from a retired local craftsman (who made wagon models). I have yet to use it!

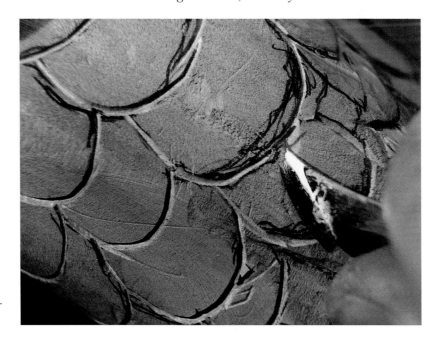

The Ashley Isles cutter to a Gonzales design, used here for step relieving.

117

PYROGRAPHY

So, finally, we come to the tooling required for the actual feather-burning process. There is only one! It is so far ahead of the rest that it is a natural choice. The basis is a range of burners produced in America under the trade name Detailmaster. They have a hard steel alloy burning tip which is sufficiently tough to be able to mark Lime wood even when cold. There are a number of profiles and my own favourites are a skew chisel, a rounded dome, and a long 'pointed' burner. You can drive the hot point in with considerable force to make nostril holes. The skew chisel cuts feather barbs, undercuts feathers and tails, and shades large scorched areas. My first purchase is still going strong after 15 years of service.

Unfortunately you have to have a different complete hand-piece unit for each profile as the heads are not detachable.

My burners are driven by a Peter Child's pyro driver which has been slightly modified to take the ¼in radio jack plug with which the Detailmasters are normally supplied.

Forget the bent wire pyrograph tools, they are far too flimsy and do not last, and one plastic box driver unit made in this country is positively dangerous.

And, until you get on to painting, that is it. We will be looking at painting equipment as we work through the processes of applying colour.

What we need to consider next is the vital question of keeping the cutting tools sharp.

My burning passion. The driver is by Peter Childs but has a ¼in radio jack plug. The burners are all Detailmaster. The two spares have never been needed!

11

GETTING AN EDGE

Few people consciously resent the time spent on sharpening tools, but many of us tend to put off the evil hour as long as possible. We have all at one time or another left the resharpening of chisels until they are so blunt that they are only usable as stone bolsters.

Constant mention has been made of the need for really sharp tools, and for years, as with many woodworkers, tool sharpening has been the bane of my life. It took precious time away from the workshop days and I suppose that in the end I really did resent it. Then with the involvement in turning I found to my total joy that you could simply zap the tool for a few seconds on a high-speed grind wheel and use it right away. If you did not get it quite right and created a little torn grain you simply burnished it away with rotary sanders. This is certainly not good enough in other areas of woodworking activity.

When I started duck carving it was a return to hours of sharpening. Fortunately, I soon found that the improvement in speed and quality of work when using very sharp tools was such that the time investment in sharpening was amply rewarded. It soon became apparent that an extra two or three minutes spent burnishing the edge on a 4,000 grit waterstone and then on a polishing mop gave me an extra hour or two's easy carving. Finding that sharpening tools was not just an unpleasant means to an end, but made an immensely valuable contribution to what I was doing made it an important subject in its own right. It became an area of study, and an interest in improving the process soon brought rewards. I think that now, with the assistance of a few friends, I have it sussed!

One thing that you learn very quickly is that you can not cut with tools that are blunt, and you certainly can not control

The bevel is not in contact and there is no flow of water up the blade (see page 126).

Now the wave runs up the blade indicating that the bevel is flat on the stone.

the incising of fine detail with tools that are anything less than razor sharp. 'Razor' is the key word. A tool for carving wood should be capable of dry shaving the hairs off your arm. As a bird carver, having to use a mallet usually indicates that you have done something wrong.

You also learn something else. Sharpening tools is a great deal more than just rubbing them on an oilstone (which is how many of us started!). First you have to have tools of the right quality. Some makers' tools sharpen better and hold their edge much longer than do others. There are significant differences between the types of steel and the degree of temper used by the various makers. Ashley Isles have tested tools for me and shown that those makes that I do not like sometimes have fractions of a percentage difference in the alloys used. They also showed me that re-tempering with a minute change in the level of temper could give huge changes in performance even on blades of poorer steel.

Next, and this is within your immediate control, there are significant differences in results between the various methods of sharpening. Thirdly, there is an almost exponentially improving pay-off between the time that you spend on sharpening and the length of time that the edge will last. Let's examine some of these contentions.

The question of favoured makes, types of steel and degrees of temper were dealt with in the last chapter, so we now need to focus upon the sharpening process itself.

The traditional method of sharpening carpentry and carving edge tools was either large, hand-turned, wet-running natural sandstone wheels, or oilstones, or a combination of the two. Then along came the slow-speed wet-wheel grinders such as the excellent Tormek. Next appeared the Japanese waterstones and many of us began to enjoy edges that we had previously not thought possible. Somewhere around about this time we also got diamond laps. Recently that great carver (and nice guy) Colin Hickman has introduced me to a high-speed grinder approach similar to that used with turning tools. This has proved to be very interesting, and has now quite changed my life.

Each method of sharpening has its own devotees, and at various times and for different reasons I still use most of them.

The huge natural sandstone wheels with the cast-iron water bath and big cranked handle, often seen in farmyards, are best sold off as antiques and the money invested in a better solution. They do give a good workable edge to axes and scythes, but as with traditional reaping with the old Father Time scythe, they belong to an age when you could afford to spend some hours of each day sharpening your tools. Oilstones too are now the province of a few dedicated traditionalists. Again, these are effective if used properly but enormously time-consuming. These are now both on my never use list.

Japanese waterstones and diamond laps do produce a keen edge quite quickly. They certainly outperform oilstones, and for a while waterstones were my mainstay; but they are also really too slow overall when you have a number of edge tools on the go. The finer grades of waterstones (4,000 and 8,000 grits) will actually produce a mirror finish without stropping or burnishing.

The two stones that I use are 800 grit for serious shaping and 4,000 for honing. They are used standing in water in a paint roller tray. However, with the Tormek available the 800 stone is now rarely used.

One face of each stone is kept for wide blades; the other face is used for gouges that are sharpened sideways – along the bevel. Small flat bevels are ground along the edge of the stone. Obviously the tools are moved right across the faces to minimize the wearing of troughs and ridges.

The problem with the 4,000 grit stone is that it is very soft and the not too infrequent accidents mean a dig in and a nasty pit in the stone. Both stones are therefore dressed at intervals with a coarse grit Devil Stone to maintain a flat surface. My first 4,000 grit stone had to be replaced due to excessive pitting.

If the tool is really blunt or damaged you do need something faster. But, overall, do not write waterstones off.

My Diamond Laps are reserved for use only on tungsten carbide-tipped turning tools, they are too slow and too expensive for use elsewhere.

For me, today, there are now two choices. First is the Tormek type grinder followed by waterstone honing and leather wheel burnishing; or the high-speed grinder approach promoted by Colin Hickman on behalf of Ashley Isles. The unit in question is a Rexon EBC 150A Grinder.

The choice is not easy. The Tormek/stone approach is aeons quicker than oilstones. With the Tormek it is easy to sharpen the edge to the correct bevel angle and the grind is in the direction of the length of the blade. The 2in-wide grind wheel makes it much easier to sharpen wider blades, and the stone is of a hard gray grit composite which resists wear and grooving. Both this wheel and the wet Japanese stones are water lubricated (and therefore run very cool).

Early models of the Tormek had a hard rubber/grit composite wheel on the left-hand end of the shaft. This was for burnishing. It was 'adequate' but very slow and never really gave a mirror finish. There is an alternative wheel available and this has a leather surface that is more effective. It is still slow and I prefer high-speed burnishing. I therefore now have a stitched Calico wheel fixed on an arbour.

This is mounted on a lathe (for convenience), is spun at 2,000rpm and is dressed with the green-coloured abrasive compound. The back of the blade is given a quick dab and then the bevel for about half a minute. A full mirror finish is quickly achieved and the cutting edge is superb. It will not require re-sharpening all day, although a revisit back to the mop before you break for lunch can put a sparkle back into the afternoon. If you use a lathe or similar to spin the mop you have to remember that you are not 'turning' and that the tool has to be offered to the far side of the mop!

Because of the width of the grind wheel and the long supporting rest, the Tormek is the ideal starting point for spokeshave blades and plane irons. The whole width of irons of up to 3in (7.5cm) or more can be ground by sliding the blade side to side, and there are jigs to facilitate this. When it comes to honing, the waterstone is first dressed flat with a Devil Stone and the blade is then applied at a slight angle so that the two corners reach the edge of the stone. The grinding/honing is then done slightly diagonally to the axis of the blade.

However else you sharpen your edge tools, it is a good idea to give them a major servicing on the Tormek once in a while. Using the wheel's jigs you can recover a perfect angle and trueness. Of course, major damage such as a chip or hitting a hidden nail may be first ground away on a high-speed dry grinding wheel, but do not forget to take the blade off the wheel at very frequent intervals and plunge it into cold water. If you ever get bluing on the edge it means that the blade has got too hot and has lost its temper. You will never get bluing on the Tormek!

So what about Colin Hickman's dry grinder? Quite simply its performance is mind-blowing! It is a high-speed grinder that is run dry, and that uses a small-

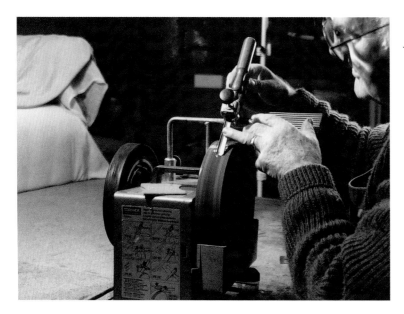

Using one of the several jigs that are available for the Tormek – here for sharpening curve bevelled gouges.

diameter pink aluminous silicate grit wheel. Here the tool is ground side-on along the line of the edge. Grinding is followed by buffing at the other end of the machine on a canvas wheel that is lightly dressed with green abrasive compound. It takes me 7–10 minutes on a single tool to achieve perfection with the wet wheels; against that is the less than half a minute to get a good edge with the Rexon method.

There is however a very special technique involved – it takes five minutes to learn. The Rexon grinder unit is fitted with a small lamp on a flexible column. The tool is offered to the wheel at right angles to the line of rotation so the grind is along the cutting edge. The lamp is positioned outboard of the tool so that the light shines down the length of the blade. The blade is first offered to the stone at a slightly shallower angle than required. In this position the light will make a shadow just beyond the blade tip. The tool is now tilted until the shadow just disappears – the bevel is now at the correct angle to lie flat on the stone. In seconds a feather burr appears along the edge of the blade – once you see this (and I have to wear a

magnifying visor), the grind is complete.

You do need good eyesight and the light shadow method works best when the ambient light is not too high. It is ideal for that dark, useless corner of the workshop.

Of course, the small diameter of the wheel on the high-speed grinder only allows limited access and is really only suited to small edge tools. It can be used on sculpting size chisels and gouges but it is totally unsuitable for spokeshave blades and draw-knives – and adzes and axes if you use these.

Obviously, with broader blades the edge has to be moved sideways (up and down the wheel) until the burr is achieved end to end; in this way you can sharpen firmer chisels of up to 1½in (4cm) wide. If the tool has a gouge form then it has to be rolled on its axis once correct contact has been established; but in all cases you use the shadow method of adjusting the grind angle.

With any typical carving tool, the approach, angle finding, and grinding takes well under five seconds. Certainly, despite the high speed there is not time for the blade to even get warm.

Once the burr has been raised on the

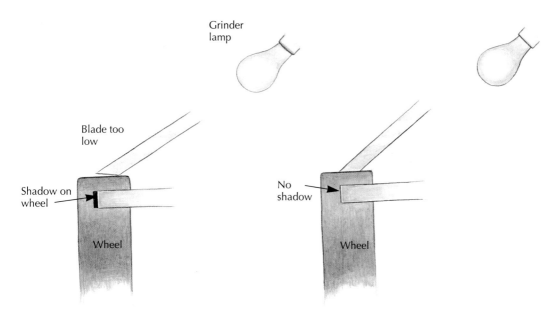

Using the shadow to set the grind angle.

blade, the tool is taken to the buffing mop. The Rexon comes with a calico buffer wheel fitted. This is very lightly dressed with green abrasive. The flat side of the blade is presented first and then the bevel. In 2–5 seconds the bevel will polish to a full mirror and the tool is ready for use.

With the blade waterstone-honed and and the edge mop-burnished, I shall have the best part of a full day's carving before re-sharpening is needed. The high-speed grinder edge, while brilliant to start with, appears to begin to fall off after three or four hours of heavy use. It may therefore need to be redone by lunch-time. Overall the dry grind is at least ten times as quick, but the edge would not be quite as 'perfect'. It would appear that there is a difference created by down or across the bevel grinding. But does it really matter? The issue is really only academic – the percentage difference in results is so minimal and is certainly not worth the required time investment!

Incidentally, how do you test for keenness? The idea of feeling it with your thumb might do for penknives and scythes but is useless at the level that we are now operating. What you feel with your thumb is not really 'sharpness' but roughness. It is the microscopic saw-like jaggedness that you are feeling. With blades of the sharpness that we require, the burnishing has removed all jaggedness and you feel nothing as the incision is made deep into your thumb. Instead, try dry-shaving the hairs on the back of your hand – if you feel no tearing as they disappear the edge *is* sharp!

However, the choice between slow wet or fast dry grinders is still not as simple as that. Most bird carvers have difficulty in sharpening one of our most frequently used tools – the Vee gouge. Some also find that they can not readily obtain a good curve on a fingernail gouge. The 'shadow line' method used by Colin totally overcomes this problem, and you can almost guarantee good results every time on any profile of tool. To me that is worth a tremendous lot as I have never once totally successfully sharpened a Vee on wet stones or the Tormek.

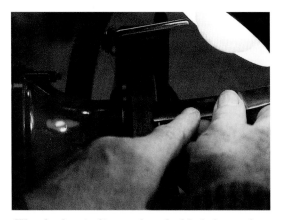

The shadow indicates that the blade has to be lifted to get the correct angle.

The micro burr is appearing indicating that the grind is complete – total time 2–3 seconds.

Buffing to get a mirror finish – another 3 seconds – and the tool is razor sharp.

A Vee gouge is sharpened in three stages. First the apex of the vee is ground. This is treated as a micro gouge – and still has its own shadow. The back of the vee is brought into contact with the wheel and the hand is raised until there is no shadow under the tip. At this stage the tool is rolled around its axis – just like a gouge. The tool is then presented so one flute is ground like a flat chisel. It is then re-presented to grind the other flute. You usually have to adjust the light to allow room for the tool handle. It is a good idea to have a 'dry run' – to position the light and offer up the tool in all three planes to check that you are getting good shadows

before you actually switch the wheel on. You will probably not get the grind right every time but it is now four out of five tries that are correct whereas I used to average about one reasonable one in ten attempts using other sharpening methods.

So I can see my Tormek, wonderful as it is, being relegated to the sharpening of plane irons, broad bevel chisels, spoke-shave blades, and draw-knives, where it will still, and forever, rule as king.

The problem in sharpening all edge tools is in maintaining the required bevel angle, this is why a Tormek regrind was recommended a few moments ago. In time even the shadow method drifts!

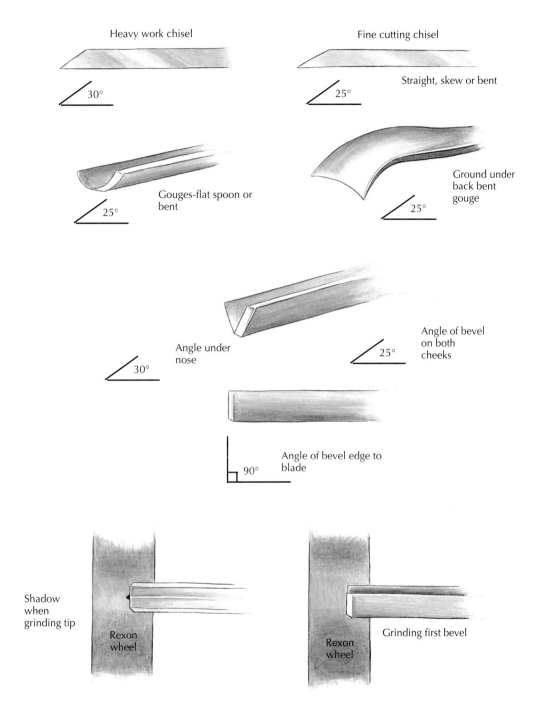

Heavy work chisel

30°

Fine cutting chisel

25°

Straight, skew or bent

Gouges-flat spoon or bent

25°

Ground under back bent gouge

25°

Angle under nose

30°

Angle of bevel on both cheeks

25°

Angle of bevel edge to blade

90°

Shadow when grinding tip

Rexon wheel

Rexon wheel

Grinding first bevel

Grind angles and sharpening Vee gouges.

It is easy to achieve and maintain whatever angle you want with the Tormek. Available for the unit is a setting gauge that enables you to set the tool rest at the right angle. The blade is then placed flat on the rest and hey presto! There are also a set of clamps and jigs that hold different patterns of blade and allow them to move side to side (and in the case of gouges to roll around their axis). These jigs present the edge at a constant preset angle to the surface of the stone. Furthermore the large diameter of the wheel means that the concave ground into the bevel is insignificant.

Although we all have our own quirks and fancies, most hold that an optimum bevel angle for carving tools is 30 degrees, possibly coming down to 25 for spoon and back gouges. My fancy is nearer 25 degrees for all with some as fine as 20 degrees. Because I never use a mallet on carving chisels, I do not need the extra mechanical strength of a 30 degree bevel.

Even without the jigs, maintaining the 30 degree bevel is not difficult on a Tormek once it has been initially established correctly. Here you do not have a light shadow to assist you, but you do have a water wave. The blade is laid on the rest and is then drawn back until the bevel is flat on the wheel. When the edge reaches the correct angle a ripple of water flows up the blade. If you get the angle too fine, there is no water scoop on top. If you get it too steep, a wave front forms at the tip and does not run up the blade (*see* page 119).

Incidentally, in passing, the DIY plane iron jigs designed for use on oil- and wetstones which have a wheel that runs on the stone are not particularly helpful. The wheel of the jig can quickly wear a trough in the stone.

Honing a draw-knife is a two-stage process. Obviously you start by grinding on the Tormek. Next the waterstone is clamped in a bench-top vice (or in a small water bath let into the top of a sawhorse).

The vice (or trough) must allow free movement of the knife handles. If the stone is not in its own bath, the surface must be sprinkled with water at frequent intervals.

My new Flexcut draw-knife referred to earlier will just angle across the Rexon wheel and buffer so it is sharpened on this. The bigger, older knives have to be done on the Tormek grind wheel, but they are now buffed on the Rexon.

Mirror honing is then again done on the mop – Rexon or lathe mounted.

Abrasive compounds for dressing mops are available in several grades. Some toolmakers will provide small sticks. Often these are coloured brown with a slight reddish hue. Unfortunately this is at variance with long-established engineering standards. At one time the colour told you precisely what metal the abrasive was designed for. Green was for tool steels, brown for brass, grey was for stainless steel and red rouge for gold, silver and pewter. It makes a considerable difference when you use the correct abrasive – too hard and you do not get as fine a finish, too soft (and too much) and you burnish on a thick black gunge.

There is finally one near insoluble sharpening problem! Two profiles of hand adzes are often used by carvers for really large pieces. One has a very shallow concave to the edge; the other is more scooped and has a deep concave. You can not sharpen this latter shape on any of the commercial, powered machines.

The answer can lie in a home-built unit. Picador make shafts, bearings, drive pulleys and other bits. One friend, Cilla, has assembled some Picador components into a multi-function sharpening and buffing station. This is driven from a 1,000-rpm washing-machine motor. The station is fitted out with various canvas mops and hard felt burnishers (some of which are on a small secondary, pulley-geared shaft) to turn at 3,000 revs. She also has a 6in-

The Rexon tool sharpening set-up showing the light set to cause a bevel shadow.

diameter grey grit wheel which, while partly boxed, has a substantial arc at the top left exposed. It was a 1in wide wheel but has been dressed with a devil stone to a radiused profile. Because of the exposed section of the wheel and the possibility that bits could fly if it shattered, it is run at the safe motor speed of 1,000. This stone can grind into quite deep concaves.

Where even this won't work it is a question of slipstones followed by a round diamond lap – and a lot of (lo'ra) time! She is known at the club, affectionately, but not surprisingly, as Slipstone Cilla.

12

SLICKS AND THE LIKE

When it comes to painting, the choice of styles is as wide as your imagination allows. The range of suitable mediums and colours is enormous. There are some traditions, but you do not have to work within these. There are some firm favourites, and it is these that we will focus upon.

Many early hunter carvers tended to rely on the few basic colours of lead house-paint that were available in the local store. Now most of the master decoyists use the finest artists' paints – normally acrylics. By today's standards, the earliest decoys were so crude that it is amazing that they fooled any other bird. But it was often the maker's choice to go for simple representations and muted colours that would weather and merge in with the background. Then, as duck carving became a competitive activity in its own right, and hunters started to collect birds, most American makers went for a much broader palette. By using the full range of artists' colours they found that they could get very close to the true colours of the birds they were portraying. They used their wooden carvings as canvases on which they could create their artistic masterpieces. Some were impressionistic, some realistic.

Some carvers choosing impressionistic styles used broad swathes of bright colour of the right hue. Others now chose to paint or stain their carvings so that they looked very similar to the mute decoys of a couple of centuries ago. A few use black, verdigris green and metallic bronze paints so that their work looks like a weathered.

antique bronze casting. At one time we had no hope of simulating the green/black iridescence of a Mallard's head – today we can add coloured glitter or use one of the wonderful interference paints and achieve startling effects.

Not all early painted representations of birds were drab. In tombs in Luxor's Valley of the Kings some wall decoration includes beautiful, sparkling paintings of geese with colours quite as bright as can be achieved with today's pigments.

So which way do you want to go? Will you follow one of the traditional approaches associated with the different styles of carving or are you going to plough a new furrow?

We will start our exploration into the question of painting not by proposing a particular style, but by looking only at colouring techniques. To give us a focus we will look first at smooth carvings – what the decoy community know as Slicks. We will examine two colouring approaches, because between them they use all the very basic techniques for applying colour and they well illustrate some fundamental principles. In the next chapter we will then consider some more advanced brush-work techniques as we consider Featherstroke painting.

The first approach to look at must be colour staining, and we will then look at flat painting – irrespective of the actual colours that we use. Realistic painting will then be dealt with in our final chapter, as this introduces other ideas.

Before we go any further there is a vital message to stress. We are going to talk of artists' colours, colour wheels, primary and secondary colours, watercolour painting, wet in wet, and we use terms more common in the art class than the carving studio. Please do not be put off. You do not have to know anything about painting and you certainly do not have to have any drawing ability at all before you start to colour bird carvings. The body, the outline, and all the details are now there. You don't have to draw anything – in fact what you are about to do is, in reality, little more than painting by numbers. You do sometimes have to control a brush to get a clear edge to a colour zone, but if you can draw a line with a pencil or paint the frame of a window in the house – then you have all the actual skills that you need. The *only* difficulty you might have is if you are seriously colour blind.

Even when you progress to painting fine detail on a realistic carving the only additional skills that you need are purely mechanical – being able to control two or three different patterns of brush stroke to make dots and fine lines as well as broad blotches.

There is one basic area of knowledge that any artist will have and with which we also need a nodding acquaintance. We all learnt at school that white light is made up of the seven basic colours of the spectrum. Many water-colour painters have a paint box with only six or seven colours – approximately similar to those of the spectrum. Some of the best photo-real colour printers now on the market have only five colour dyes and one black. With these they can reproduce any of the millions of colours, hues and shades that make up a true-to-life colour picture. Neither the water-colour artist nor the photo printer have white – they rely on the whiteness of the paper. Many artists do not have a black in their kit – they make 'black' with dark brown and dark blue.

The three basic primary colours are red, yellow and blue – and that is all that some colour printers have. Mix roughly equal quantities of any two primaries, and you get the secondaries – orange, green and purple. Vary the percentages in the mix and you get shades.

So why then, when you go into an art shop do you see 200 different colours of paint in a single maker's range of tubes, or

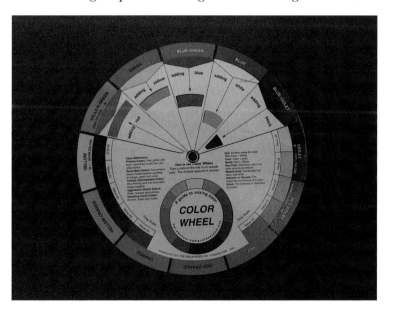

A useful gadget to aid in colour mixing – the artist's colour wheel.

as many as 500 different shades of pastels? There are two answers. First, laziness of the artist – many find it better to let the paint manufacturers do the mixing for them. Secondly, some media are very difficult to mix – you can blend pastels, but it is not easy and the results are muddy. The more opaque the media the more muddy the mix. To overcome the problem they therefore use a ready-mixed blend of the right colour and apply this direct to their canvas. Watercolours (and stains and dyes) are completely transparent and mix superbly. So a good water-colour painter may have only eight different tubes, whereas an oil painter may need two dozen or more.

Mix any two primaries and you get a good secondary whatever the media. Mix more than two and you tend to get a muddy hue. Browns and a good 'black' are easy to produce by mixing – black is dark brown with dark blue. Making white is impossible!

Colour-staining is the only one of the whole range of painting techniques where the carving is not first primed. You want the grain of the wood to show through. As you have no underlying white 'canvas' on which to paint, you have to dilute the stain and apply less of it to get lighter shades. You also want the stain to penetrate the wood and give 'depth' to the colour – indeed, the more natural the wood is and the less it is burnished with fine abrasives, the better.

Whatever the medium (water or spirit-based) which carries the pigment, stains and dyes are best thought of as water-colours. With a kit of only six or seven colours you can produce most of the hues that you need. The basic kit marketed by Liebron is a good starting outfit.

You can mix your colours in one of two ways. One is to mix them on a palette (saucers or jam-jar lids, and so forth) and then to test the blend on a scrap of wood. The other is to mix them directly as you apply them to the bird.

The watercolour technique known as 'wet in wet' is simply this. First paint the area that you wish to work on with the highlight or lightest colour but take this wet wash over the whole of the area. Now while it is still wet take your darker colour (possibly a shadow) and starting at the darkest area run colour in with a wet brush. Next take the surplus paint off the brush and working from the dark area

 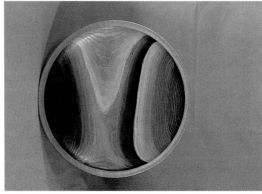

The work of Jan Sanders, the country's top wood colourist. Here turned vases are dyed with a single colour and gold is rubbed into the grain to emphasize the figuring. The brilliance of the wooden bowl shows the full potential of wood dyes, and this could very effectively be applied to carved ducks.

towards the lighter, blend the colours together. Simple! With only two colours you have produced a continuing gradation which has given you in effect thousands of different shades.

You can only add detail if it is darker than the underlying colour, so with stains (and watercolours) you always work from light to dark. There is a trick that watercolour painters sometimes use and this can be useful to you on things like eyes. They have a rubber-based solution which is painted on before any colour is applied. This dries and resists any paint or stain that you apply over the top. When the whole work is dry you simply rub off the mask with a finger. The wonder liquid? – Masking Fluid! (from any art shop).

The great beauty of staining is that you can still see the grain of the wood through the colour. It is obvious that the piece is of carved wood. Clearly for this to be effective you do want wood that has a good figure, but equally the more absorbent the better. Lime and Jelutong meet the latter criterion, but are characterless in terms of grain. Oak and ash responds beautifully to staining, resinous pine does not!

Whatever other form of colour that you use the carving has first to be primed – this helps the paint to stick to the wood. Therefore for both flat and feather-stroke painted birds apply a coat of sanding sealer and flatten this down. Next, use a thick-bodied primer of a suitable nature for the paint that you will be applying. Today, your paint will almost certainly be acrylic. Most carvers now use student grades of acrylic paint – they are quite a bit cheaper than artists quality, and again most use tube colour although a few prefer to work with small pots or jars of a paint of a more liquid consistency.

The best primer for slicks that are to be painted with acrylic colours is a thick acrylic gesso. This offers the advantage of filling small surface blemishes. Apply a coat, let it dry and then give it another coat that is also allowed to dry. The surface is next cut back with 400 grit wet or dry used with water and finally a more dilute working coat is applied.

There is one huge advantage with acrylic paint – it air-dries quite quickly. The process can also be greatly accelerated by judicious use of a hair-dryer (or electric

Acrylic paints (and gesso) can be dried very quickly with a hair dryer. Here a paint stripper is used on low-heat setting.

blower paint-stripper set on low). Take great care not to overheat and cause the surface to blister. Using a dryer the whole multi-layer priming process can be achieved in about 20 minutes.

Acrylic paints are opaque, hence there is no showing through of the base colour. They, and oil paints, are used entirely differently from watercolour. Here, most of the mixing is done on the palette. More important, the colouring sequence is also reversed. It is the dark areas and shadows that are blocked in first and you then build up the lighter zones finishing with the highlights. You also normally let an area dry before you overpaint it. So again the hair dryer is often called into service. Certainly before painting a hard edge to a colour you let the colour that it abuts or overlies dry first.

Of course you do not always want a hard edge. If you closely inspect a live bird there is usually just a little softening where two colours appear to be meeting in a clear margin. Working to the rule, you will be applying the darker colour first. Do not just paint up to the join line with the next colour zone but carry on with the dark colour well over the line. Let the paint dry (30 seconds with the hair dryer). Now paint on the main body of the lighter zone. As you come up to the margin take up a stiff bristled dry brush, dip the tip into a little paint and lightly dab this across the marginal line.

You can achieve almost all that you ever want in painting slicks with about twelve to fifteen tubes of paint. No doubt however, like all of us, you will end up with more. The argument is that the more colours you have the more subtle the effects that you can achieve, and the less you actually need to know about the finer points of colour mixing. It is interesting that with almost all painters (of birds and canvases) the more experience they gain, the smaller becomes the range of colours that they buy.

So let's take a look at a basic kit. Those starred are what you should start *and end up* with! The unstarred items are the ones that you will find useful and that will appear in your paintbox until you learn to do without them!

WHITES:	*Titanium White *Unbleached Titanium (not always available)
EARTH:	*Raw Umber *Burnt Umber *Raw Sienna *Burnt Sienna *Yellow Ochre
GREENS:	*Phalto Green *Hookers Green Olive Green Viridian
BLUES:	*French Ultramarine Cobalt Blue
REDS:	*Bright Red *Alizarine Crimson Venetian Red or Red Iron Oxide
YELLOWS:	*Cadmium Yellow Medium Cadmium Orange
DARK:	*Paynes Grey *Ivory Black (only as a bird painter)
SPECIALS:	Dioxazine Purple Colour metal powders, or *Iridescent or Interference Gold Iridescent or Interference Green Iridescent or Pearlescent Purple
MEDIUMS etc.:	Cryla Matt Medium and Varnish Liquitex Matte Medium (used in Featherstroke)

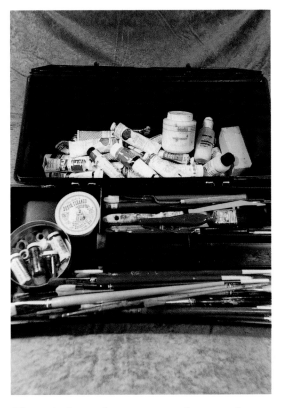

The paintbox – far too many colours and several never-used brushes.

Incidentally, the best paintbox is a plastic tool-box as bought in motor accessory shops. You can go for the multi-tray concertina if you like but most find a simple box with one compartmented lift-out tray quite adequate. The paint tubes, bottles of medium and varnish and so on are kept in the body of the box and the brushes and ancillaries in the tray.

Acrylic paints are water-based and can therefore be thinned out with water if you require a paint that will not show brush marks. However, most users of acrylic tube paints do not use water but instead use a little medium, and for this the Cryla Matt Medium is recommended. This keeps the paint moist while in use and assists in the 'spreadability'. Once the painting is completed the whole surface is also given two or three coats of the medium that dries to form a completely transparent, matt 'varnish' – this gives protection against bruising and water penetration.

You should have good brushes and do need to take care of them. The hog bristle brushes used by many artists are too coarse for most duck painting, but equally you do not need to go to the full and fearfully expensive real sable that water-colourists favour. Daler's dalon brushes of artificial hair are a reasonable compromise. Dalon is described as the closest artificial rival to sable. Daler also make a Cryla range designed specifically for use with acrylic paints. Some nylon brushes are also quite nice.

Several years ago I went on a duck-painting course with a great American decoyist called Beebe Hopper. She it was who coined the phrase 'Featherstroke Painting'. Most of her students bought one of her kits of brushes. There were four in the box – all were of pure red sable, and good as Dalon is you can tell the difference. The kit offered a size 10 and an 8 'Kat's Tongue' brush, their tip profile being gently rounded like a finger or thumbnail. There was then a size 10 Shader – this has a squared chisel end. The fourth was a size 0 Liner – best described as half a dozen long hairs on a stick!

The nearest UK equivalent to the Kat's Tongues are some of our Filberts, although many makers' filberts tend to be more pointed than rounded. While I use the Hooper kit more than any others, I do find larger sizes of brush are often useful so I have a 12 and 14 Dalon Series 33 (Filberts). There is then a ¾in nylon square-ended flat brush that is used for gesso and varnish, a round and a square-tip Bristlewhit bristle brush for dry work and a Dalon Fan for some feather tipping processes. The other 20 or so brushes (many with virgin bristles) that fill out the box must be for window dressing!

133

Beebe Hopper's sable brush set and book.

To complete the kit is a palette and a small palette knife for mixing colours. Palettes come in two forms, you can make one and buying the other will not break the bank. The first form is the conventional board that you have seen in pictures of artists at work. It is a heavily varnished Mahogany or 6mm plyboard with a thumb hole, and is shaped to sit neatly on the hand. There is even a recess to allow you to also hold a number of brushes. Beautiful yes, but for you a waste of time. You will be sitting at a bench to do your painting and therefore do not need to carry paint to a canvas. All you need is a sheet of glass, or a well-varnished board. The second form of palette is primarily of use to a water-colour painter. They have a number of small wells around the periphery of a central mixing zone. They can be obtained from any art shop, are made in China of china, and are quite cheap. Either style will do and it is a matter of preference. When bird painting I like the piece of glass.

It is a good idea to develop a discipline over use of the palette. First is to always put the same colours in the same positions. This prevents you from having to search around for a colour, and it means that you can often pick up a touch without even looking. Second is to only put out those colours that you are going to be working with in the next few moments. Acrylic paint starts to dry the moment it is squeezed from the tube and some of the rarer colours are too expensive to waste.

The last item of kit is a pot of Brush Cleaner soap. Paint is never allowed to dry on a brush (popping them in water keeps the paint moist during use). When the job is completed the brushes are washed in tepid running water and are then cleaned on the soap. Finally they are dried out by gently squeezing back to the proper shape using a piece of kitchen roll. On fine brushes you should neither use very hot water nor aggressive paint solvents.

With the kitting up out of the way, let's get on with the first bird. It is a Slick – primed, white and smooth. There is probably primer over the eyes, but don't worry about that, we can clean that off with a scalpel later.

Using an HB or 2B lead pencil draw on the margins of all colour zones – use a single line for hard edges and a zig-zag for blended areas.

Where you start the painting will depend to some extent on your approach to carving. Earlier we mentioned Carver's Screws. If you have your bird mounted on one of these, preferably of the ball-head variety, you can now do the painting without having to handle (hold) the bird. In this case it is a good idea to start with the head and work systematically back, through each zone, towards the tail. I do not use a screw and therefore while painting the body I tend to hold the bird by the head or neck. I therefore paint the head last with the bird sitting on the bench.

You are of course, at the moment, painting only large swathes of flat colour on a slick. You may therefore paint all the blocks of one colour, then those of the next colour and so on. In this case start with the blacks, then the browns, blues, reds, yellows and finally the whites. This keeps the highlights both physically and visually 'on the top'.

Squeeze out onto your palette a little of the pigments that you are going to use next. With the knife take appropriate quantities of the colours that you want to mix and blend these in the central area. If you want a wetter consistency, drip on a quantity of matt media and stir the lot together.

Most of the broad areas will be applied with a filbert. Paint the edge of the area first and then with broad strokes fill in the middle. Usually it is best with the earlier colour applications to go over the pencil line. Overlying colours are then painted with more care to firm up colour-zone edges. First define the edge this time using the tip of the filbert to make as clean a line as you require. From there on it really is, as was suggested earlier, almost painting by numbers.

To paint accurate detail artists use a Mahl Stick. This is a cane with a knob head which is rested on a dry part of the canvas to support the brush hand. With quick drying (or heat-dried) acrylics you do not need a stick. The fleshy edge of the hand can be supported direct on a dry part of the bird and your brushstrokes are then made by flexing the fingers. In this way, and with no 'art' training at all, you can paint very precise detail.

Drawing fine lines with a liner, or the even longer pointed Rigger brush is not difficult but it is worth practising. There are two movements that you will need – one is an even line (straight or curved), the second is a shorter line that ends in a point.

The first is done with the brush point resting on the bird with a slight bend to the bristles; the fingers are fully extended. The line is started by drawing in the fingers, and at the same time the whole hand is drawn back sliding it on the surface of the bird. To get a long continuous line you need to start with the brush well charged with paint but with the point in very light contact. Tip pressure is now increased slightly as the brush sheds its load.

The short, point-ending line, starts with a lesser bend in the brush tip but this time, as the fingers are drawn back, they also lift the brush tip. It is a distinct upward flicking motion as though trying to get the brush tip into the palm of the hand.

You do not need to practise this on a bird. Take a little paint of any colour, add sufficient media (or water) to give you a paint that will properly charge the brush and practise the movement on a sheet of paper. Experiment with different consistencies of paint, but concentrate on the finger movement. You will quickly develop the knack. When you do start on a bird it is a good idea to take a flick or two on a

The main areas of colour have been blocked in on this male Merganser slick. Edges have now to be softened and detail painted in.

A Carolina Wood Duck. Although basically a simple painted slick, some feather detailing has been done.

corner of the palette before you make the first on-bird mark.

The most basic of Slicks use only the most elementary of painting techniques. Each zone of colour is flat – there is no light or shade, no shading or shadows. If it is a red zone, it is one colour of red and so on. With simple slicks it is unusual to show feather detail although you may have one or two dark-coloured lines to hint at two or three of the primary wing feathers. You do not normally show vermiculation – the tiny lines across all the pouch feathers of some birds. The sides of a male Mallard are a classic example.

Adding some colour differentiation can make a big difference to the appearance of a bird. So now our flat zone of colour – say a bright red – may start as a slightly orange red, shade to a bright clear red and then veer towards a crimson. Often brown zones show subtle colour variations and whites can go from sunshine white (the merest trace of added Cadmium Yellow) to a soft bluish gray (added Paynes Grey).

To make graduated colours take first to the mixing area of your palette some of the main colour pigment. Next put either side of this a small quantity of the colours that you wish to add. With your palette knife draw a little of the added colour into the edge of the main body colour and just mix a little. Again drip on a little medium.

This time paint the main colour central zone first. Next, with the brush tip pick up a little of the partial mixture and start to work outwards. With your next pick up go for a little more of the added colour. Do the final mixing on the bird blending in the colours as you go. Don't forget that although two colours mix nicely, if you start to introduce a third, you are taking the first step towards producing mud.

Our next development will be to add detail and to define a lot of the feathering – all using paint. It is now time to read the next chapters.

— 13 —

FEATHERSTROKING

Featherstroke painting is a whole different scene – not so much in the techniques of painting, but in the appearance of the end results. It does however rely on some slightly more advanced brushwork. It also makes a great deal of use of the idea of laying one colour on another so that the underlying colour can still show through. The most significant aspect is that you now paint on the feathers (or at least an impression of some of the more significant feathers) so that their pattern and shape can be clearly seen.

Done well it is extremely effective and adds greatly to the bird's appeal. As was implied earlier, it is not actually realistic! Looking at a real bird you can often see the distinct outline of only a very few of the major feathers; those of the upper scapulars and the pockets may have a colour pattern but absolutely no distinct shape or outline. In featherstroke you often draw a line to show the outline – this is highly artificial. As with carving the feathers you now show much more of each feather than the real overlap would reveal in life. You often use a distinctive shade around the margins of the feathers and this is applied in a way to simulate the ends of the barbs. Clearly this emphasizes the outline of your artificial feathers.

Overall a lot more detail is indicated. As was mentioned in the last chapter, many birds have what is known as vermiculation. This may cover much of the pockets, it also often occurs on the neck and breast. If you examine a vermiculated feather it is quite amazing. Let's say it has a greyish-white body colour. It is then marked with a series of very fine parallel wavy lines. These lie at right angles to the quill and may only be 1mm wide and 2mm apart. Sometimes the colour line is strong and on other birds only faint. Seen in a mass on the side of a bird they produce a shimmer of lines tracing from the top of the pocket down to the underside of the bird.

Sometimes the vermiculation lines are drawn on with a waterproof drawing pen, more often they are applied in various ways using a brush. All the other detail and feather impressions are made by brush; this means that the painter needs an understanding and a developed skill, but these are not difficult to acquire. Yes, we are now stepping beyond painting by numbers, but a couple of days of trial and practice will bring you up to speed.

We already have all the paints, brushes and equipment that are needed. We have already mixed the paints and got them to the required consistency; and we have already developed two of the most fundamental of the required skills – that of painting a line and of flicking up the brush stroke. You certainly already know where the different feather groups lie and the shapes of the various feathers. So let's give it a go!

The body is primed just as you did for a flat-painted Slick. Next, the main areas are coloured but the colour is now rarely applied flat. Much more mixing is used, but this time the painted area is not brush-blended to an even gradation. The brush-fuls of paint may now each be a slightly different shade and this is more dabbed-on rather than brushed so that the dabs retain the different colour. Obviously we avoid over-emphasizing the 'blotchy' contrasts. Some depressions and lines will probably have been carved in, but if not these now have to be indicated in paint. There may be an undulation on a wing fold, so a little Paynes Grey is added to the colour to indicate a shadow. It is not normal to paint artificial shadows on the underside of the body and so forth, but some colour variation will break up the basic flatness. The natural light falling on your painted carving will do the rest.

Edges between zones are softened. This is achieved by applying the first colour, letting it dry and then putting on the second. As you get to the margin the brush carrying the second colour is charged with very little paint. It is squeezed on the palette to nearly dry. The tip is now dabbed over the edge of the underlying colour, the strokes becoming ever lighter the further you move out over the edge. In this way an increasing amount of the undercolour shows through.

Sometimes the overlying colour is added as a gradually disappearing haze.

To do this, again allow the undercolour to dry. Next, paint the main area of the second colour but now as you come to the edge clean the brush and charge it with medium and only the merest touch of pigment. The medium will look milky as applied but it dries to total transparency leaving only a trace of the added pigment that now fades to nothing again allowing increasing show-through of the under-lying paint.

According to the approach that you choose, you may next add the vermiculation or leave this process until later. We could call the method used at this stage as the wet method – the other, where we paint or draw on lines later, would then be the 'dry' one.

The wet method is very effective. In the list of paints and equipment in the last chapter one listed item was a specific make of Matte Medium – Liquitex. This brand has a gel-like consistency that makes it ideal. Paint the body colour of the zone with whatever grading or variation you think appropriate. Let this dry. Now, working on a small area at a time (the media tends to dry quickly), mix in a

The back feathers painted on a smooth-carved hen Merganser.

Beebe Hopper on a visit. Here with a group of students in Norfolk.

little of the vermiculation line colour (often a grey or brown) and apply a quantity of the mix to the bird using a broad filbert. Immediately, starting at the front of the zone with the handle of the brush out towards the head, push the coloured media into little waves. Each wave will provide a concentration of the pigment while the troughs between will be void, exposing the full body colour underlay. The mix dries quickly and the medium shrinks leaving tiny ridges of colour – the lines of vermiculation. By adjusting the quantities of pigment the lines can be made strong or faint. You can break, bend or pattern the lines and by pushing from the front you can get a defined feather-like curve to each section. When you first try the technique you may find it a little awkward to start with as you adjust the strength of the mix and practise making 'waves', but skill develops very quickly. In the end you will find the approach simple but extremely effective.

It is on the top of the back of the bird – the folded wings and the tail – where we normally paint on more distinct feathers; although on some species other areas may have feathers that themselves have clear marking thus requiring more definition.

Top-side feathers, particularly the larger ones (tail, primary, secondary and lower scapulars) are usually lined. This means that any predominant overall zone colour is applied and dried before you paint in the outline of each feather with thin lines. A quill line may also be drawn in. From here each feather is painted separately. First apply any bands that vary from the main body colour. This can sometimes mean a series of profiled bands of different colours.

Begin with the colour bands that come out to the edge. The brush for this task is what Beebe calls the Shader. It is a fairly narrow brush, 8–10mm wide, that comes to a chisel point. Because the hairs are fairly short they are also stiffer. Well-charged with paint you can produce a strong hard edge. Using the flick stroke with a 'dry' brush (minimum paint charge) you get a broken edge and a simulation of barbs. Hence the edge of the feather may be blocked in with body colour and then when dried a lighter colour flick adds a barb overlay. Each successive inner band is flick overlain on the previous band. Finally the original quill line is retraced with a liner brush.

On some birds the pocket feathers also

139

Various vermiculated and spotted feathers.

Various sable and hog's hair brushes, and the strokes that they can make. The large filbert (top right) is the most widely used.

140

have banded colour patterns – the hen Mallard and the cock Pheasant have some very distinctive zones. The hen Mallard's pocket feathers are almost identical to the tertials and some of the scapulars. These are dealt with in exactly the way outlined above for primaries and secondaries.

There is one important difference, the outline profile of pocket and flank feathers is not usually drawn in with a defined line. The edge is indicated by the tip of a flick brushstroke using a filbert.

Few brushes are as versatile as a good quality filbert. Applying a well-charged brush flat, the tip can be drawn sideways to provide a broad band with a very clear hard edge. Used with the brush held vertically and only the very tip in contact it can be moved sideways to produce a reasonably fine line. Applied flat and drawn back slightly it will produce a nice rounded feather shape. But that is only the start.

Used 'dry' with a light touch and flick it will give a good simulation of the barbed tip of a feather's edge. By fanning the tip the feather can be widened and the barbs spread. This requires that the brush is pushed vertically down onto the palette (right down to the ferrule) when the bristles will fan out – provided it is not clogged with too much pigment. By touching the edges of the fan on the palette they can be pushed in slightly to control the width and profile of the fan itself. A flick stroke with a brush prepared in this way gives a very effective simulation of a feather.

I keep a couple of different sizes of filbert specifically for this sort of fanning. They are always pushed down and bent the same way round so that they have now developed an almost permanent kink. Again, it is a good idea to practise filbert flicking.

It is at this stage that you apply 'dry' vermiculation. You have two options – both are very tedious! Using a fine liner brush, or better still a water-colourist's long Rigger, and wet paint of the appropriate colour and shade, the thousands of vermiculation lines are painted on – each one individually! The Rigger brush was developed originally for painting the rigging on pictures of sailing ships. It is very fine (although it comes in three sizes)

Working on a pair of Redheads. The male is complete. The outlines of the feathers have been painted on the hen – these lines will disappear as the colour fill is applied.

141

The completed pair of Featherstroke painted Redheads.

The vermiculations on this Featherstroke Mallard were drawn on with a waterproof lining pen. The quite effective iridescence has been lost under the electric light.

and the length of bristle provides a reasonable paint reservoir.

The alternative is to draw the lines on with a drawing pen. These can be obtained with various point sizes and in a number of different colours. I find that the colours are often too intense, particularly the blacks, and they do not tone in with the rest of the bird.

Several birds have a sheen to their feathers that create beautiful effects.

Sometimes these can be seen in a single feather, but often they can only be seen on a live bird that is catching the light in a particular way. In some instances the colour appears to be a pigment in the feather, on others it is clearly a schiller-ization effect when something breaks up the light and what you see is a sort of prismatic or rainbow effect. Whichever it is does not matter, our problem is to reproduce the effect in our painting.

The head of a Mallard male is a dark green. In flat paint terms the body colour is Hookers Green and the cheek highlights may have a touch of Cadmium Yellow. There are, down the base of the neck, areas that are almost black. This is achieved by adding a little Alizarine Crimson to the green. However, there are areas on the cheeks and the top of the head where the light picks up a certain level of iridescence. In bright sunlight and in spring plumage it can almost look like a bright green light. Other birds have purple zones and a few a blue patch that reacts in a similar way.

There are three ways of reproducing iridescence and all require a delicate touch. At one time we used to blend a little gold paint into the highlight/body colour mix that was then painted on. It worked, but not very well. Then along came metallic 'glitter' powders that could be obtained at some of the best art shops. They were available in a range of colours and the green and purple were very useful. Here the body colour and the highlights were painted on, then the tip of the brush was dipped into the powder and this was dab applied on top of the still wet paint. Finally along came a range of iridescent or interference paints that have an opal-like powder mixed in with the pigment. The trouble with the latter is that the main pigment may not be what you require and you have to adjust this by adding in other colours.

The problem with the powder is that the more you brush it the more the flakes become covered in paint and the sparkle is lost. Similarly, the more you mix in and the more you work the iridescent paints the greater the loss of the required effect. So, put simply, do not incorporate them or use them for body colour; wait until the highlights are on; now add the interference to the surface of the highlight; there should be minimum brushing and *no* mixing! If all else fails, let the body-colour dry and then apply the glitter in a thin film of medium – now you can brush it out as much as you like. Unfortunately, for me, this makes it look 'painted on'.

Next clean up the eyes. You may wish to add a line or two to simulate eyelids, and you may have to add a dot or two of paint to fill in a recess or hide the plastic wood. The main job is to scrape the paint off the glass bead. A pointed scalpel will do the job well, and should not mark the glass.

You have been sitting for some time, intensely concentrating, with your eyes only inches away from the piece that you are working on. By now your head is probably swimming and you are only seeing 'imperfections' – lines that are too thick, feather flicks that look like blotches, flat zones of colour that need differentiation, and a score of other defects. Get up and walk away from it.

But, don't go too far! Turn and look at the bird from 2–3m (6–10ft) away – doesn't it look wonderful? Put it on a table under a lamp and stand back and look at it. I can guarantee that you will like what you see!

14

LIFELIKE

Work of the ultimate quality (and I know that mine is nowhere near that – yet) can fool you. It certainly has caught me out on a couple of occasions. Quite recently, at one big agricultural show, there was a stand displaying a number of birds – it took me a long time before I finally established that it was a carver's stand and not a taxidermist's. Interestingly, the problem was made more difficult by the fact that two of the twelve birds on display were indeed stuffed. Unfortunately you could not get close enough to poke them.

There are many details that make carvings of this nature special. We have already looked at all the basic elements of carving, and there are now only a few finer points to consider, but we do need to add significantly to what has already been said about painting in the last two chapters.

In terms of the carving we need a much greater level of subtlety and a much stronger focus upon detail and realism. In this sense both the carving and the painting have to be much more realistic and much less broad-band impressionistic.

When we were discussing the carved representation of feathers it was suggested that we carve an outline around each feather – sometimes even relieving it by undercutting the outer edge. We also burnt on a quill and then incised barbs that radiated out from the quill shaft. It was pointed out that while we were emphasizing a realistic feather shape and construction, what we were really doing was being very impressionistic. In life you see so little of each feather that (with the exception of the wing and back feathers)

it does not look like a feather at all! In relation to beaks and eyes we almost went the other way – we gave an impression of what they were like but did this by carving the minimum amount of detail. We may even have used burnt lines rather than wood modelling to show detail such as eyelids.

With painted realistic birds we almost go the other way. We carve every line and wrinkle, bump and depression around the eyes, the beak and the legs; every detail is made three-dimensional. When it comes to the feathers we may (or may not) reduce the detailing and only carve in an impression of the overall lie of the barbs. Certainly it is only the wing, tail and scapulars that are likely to have a defined outline or any significant undercutting. As we saw on birds destined for realistic painting we may carve an impression of the lie of the feather barbs with a series of fine edged burrs, and we then may or may not further define the barbs, undercutting and breaks with the pyrograph tool. It is very much a question of personal preference, because done properly either style can be wonderfully lifelike once it is properly painted.

Looking at the work of top carvers you will see huge variations. Realistic birds by different carvers are distributed along a spectrum where at one end there is a very impressionistic surface marking merely hinting at a feather-like surface, right through to the other end where the feathers as they really look in life are faithfully reproduced. At this end we aim for a level of accurate representation that

Feather painting practice using watercolour paints. This is a very useful exercise particularly for identifying the difficulty of painting white feathers.

Here acrylic paint has been applied to a styrene study Ruddy Duck to give some light relief to the finely carved, and very realistic feather detail.

is more an engineering drawing than an artist's painting! This means that each feather is shown, but they have no clear outline, the barbs are not beautifully organized but are ruffled, with many breaks, and they have straight sections, curls and quiffs. The 'outline' of the feather is not defined by any line but can be seen by the boundary between two sets of barbs oriented in different directions.

Can we now then summarize feather-carving styles before moving on to how we are going to colour them – the two subjects overlap.

Impressions of feathers for painting may be achieved by repeated gouging with sharp-edged milling cutter discs or mushroom-profiled stones. The finer the abrasive the smoother and more burnished the mark. Milling tools can give a roughness or 'fluffiness' that is closer to the texture of real feathers. The effect that the barbs are radiating out from a central quill is created by moving the cutter in a series of semi-circular arcs. A shallower incision but following a similar layout may be made with a pyrograph. In both of these approaches the outline of the feather is not specifically defined with an incised or burnt line.

In contrast, impressionistic feathers often do have a defined outline. This outline may be carved or burnt. A stylized layout is adopted where the feather is represented with a central quill and the barbs are impressed and can be seen radiating out from that quill. Much more of the feather is shown than you see on a real bird and it is these clearly defined feathers that make the unpainted carving look so effective. Sometimes the feather does not have a separate carved or burnt outline but the edge of the feather is made obvious because it must be at the boundary where barbs going in one direction clearly overlie those going in another direction.

In a feather-burnt finish bird there may be a small step defining the overlay of one feather over another. This may be emphasized by undercutting; and this may even be carried on down the side pocket and under the larger breast feathers. On a carved bird that is to be painted you may still have undercutting on wing and the larger scapular feathers, but this approach

146

is used much more sparingly on all other areas covered by smaller, softer feathers. If a step is carved initially it is then rounded over or even faired off before it is burnt. Certainly in this case an outline line is not actually burnt in.

You may recall the quotation from the Betty Edwards book. 'In nature there is no such thing as a line, there is just a boundary between two planes.' This is exactly what you are doing here. You are not defining the feather by a (wholly unnatural) line, but you are establishing two planes, and there is now an 'obvious' boundary between them.

Where the bird has been pyrographed there will be loose charcoal in each burnt groove. If the pyrography was to be left exposed, you were given the option of brushing this out or fixing it in place with some form of dressing. If the bird is to be painted it is best to get rid of the charcoal. This is done by brushing fairly vigorously with a brass-bristled suede brush.

One of the first problems that you face when you start to paint a carving, is that it is very easy to fill the lines of the carving with paint. It does not take very much paint to turn a finely pyrographed marked bird into a slick because you have clogged up the fine lines and re-created a smooth surface.

If you try to solve this problem by incising the lines more deeply the results look very unnatural. What we have to do is to apply the paint in a manner that will accommodate the fineness of the line.

The first thing is to use very thin paint. The colour on realistic birds is not applied in just one or two coats but is built up in multiple coats of very thin washes. This achieves three things. First it avoids the clogging of the lines of the fine carving; secondly it gives the colour an apparent depth; and thirdly it allows you to overlay colours such that an undercolour can show through. It is this showing through that gives the impression of depth, but much more it helps you to achieve shading and subtlety and to get away totally from the swathes of flat colour.

We now come to a definite choice between two schools. One group, by far the largest, starts by covering the bird with a uniform white primer. Most use an acrylic gesso.

The second group consists primarily of those who burn the feathers in with a pyrograph (they may or may not have first

A smug Kingfisher – the envy of all fishermen! A beautiful piece of work by Judith Nicoll.

147

carved or burr-gouged feather impressions). With burning you automatically get dark colours and natural shading. This is not entirely obliterated under layers of paint but is left to add depth. It is not easy to get the effect absolutely spot-on, but it can work extremely well. Obviously you can not now prime with an opaque white gesso.

What is used is spirit and lacquer-based sealers that will penetrate into the wood. Even sanding sealer, that has been left standing so the filler has precipitated out, is quite effective. Be careful however, some sealers are of too thick a consistency and need diluting (often with methylated spirits or denatured alcohol). If you are trying this approach, you do not brush away the loose charcoal.

Even if your first painted bird is done using the gesso approach, it is worth subsequently trying the second method and seeing how you get on with it.

So, back to gesso. The gesso must be cut right back with water such that you may have to apply a couple of coats to see any effect at all. Do not worry about achieving an overall flat whiteness unless your feather incising has been strong and deep. The fewer and thinner the coats of gesso, the better.

All subsequent colours must be applied in the same way. Acrylics have to be used by mixing each with a lot of water (rather than medium) and applying each colour in two or three washes – rather like watercolours. You will find that some colours can be reduced to near transparency and others to a useful translucence. Very few pigments *have* to be applied in a fully opaque form.

There is a very fine line. If you like using really dilute washes, those that are almost of watercolour consistency, you may find it better to adopt the watercolour technique of starting with the highlights and then feeding in the darker and shadow zones. You will find that acrylics are sufficiently different from watercolours so that you can not use all the watercolour techniques – for example, wet in wet (flooding a new colour into a zone wet with the first colour) does not work. You therefore normally dry one colour off and then apply a light wash of the second colour over the appropriate zones whether you are doing highlights first or last.

A few carvers have found it better to use an air brush! The air brushes used by graphic artists are expensive and you will only be able to justify one of these if you are going to take up bird-making in a big way. But there is a much more reasonable approach available to the hobbyist. Here a simplified 'brush' is used, and this is attached by a small feed-hose to an 'aerosol' can of carbon dioxide propellant.

The beauty of an air brush is that you can apply the paint in the finest of mists. Because of the atomization given by the brush, you do not get clogging of the fine details even when using a fairly strong, opaque mix of the colours. The other huge advantage of the air brush is that you can get beautifully controlled gradation of colour between one zone and the next. You can give each area a natural but soft edge.

There are two significant disadvantages. First there is a definite skill to using an air brush. If you have been a car spray graffiti artist you may have just a little of the necessary skill! If you have not practised on cars or walls, then you will now start on a steep learning curve. The spraying distance and the continued movement of the air brush are critical – as they are in car spraying. In addition, with an air brush, the flow of the air and the addition of the paint have to be precisely regulated and controlled (and this takes you way beyond graffiti skills). You start the air first and then gradually add the paint into the

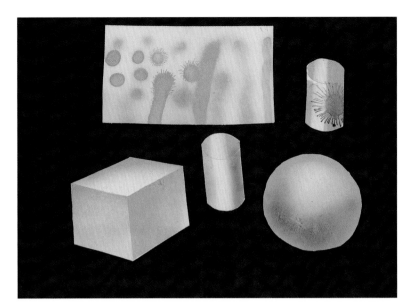

airstream. On the cheaper, more simple brushes these two actions are achieved through a single button. Typically, as you start to press the finger button the air starts, then as you depress it further this also opens the paint valve. As you take your finger off, the reverse happens, paint stops first then the air. Some early brushes had separate finger buttons for each of the two functions.

The better-quality guns still have a single button, but it has a distinct double action. Pushing the button down starts the air, then applying a little backward pressure starts the paint flow. Control of the force of the air blast and of the paint flow is greatly facilitated and much more accurate.

There are two forms of air-brush media that could interest you. Colours for air brushes are available either as inks – that are usually transparent – or as pigmented acrylics that are going to be more opaque. It is possible to also use the best quality of acrylic tube paints, and to water dilute these to a consistency that the brush can manage. This is not recommended how-ever, as the brushes are very sensitive to

clogging. Some spray paint comes as powders which are usually mixed with water; some come in concentrated liquid form in jars or pots – this also has to be diluted with water; and some, also in jars, is sold in workable dilution.

Obviously the inks give you some of the same possibilities as do wood stains or dyes.

Because of the nature of opaque acrylics, and the misted overlay of edges, you can with an air brush start with either the shadows or the highlights and then overlay lights or darks as required. Most graphic artists tend to start with the darks and shadows.

The biggest disadvantage that beginners find with air brushes is not caused by the mechanical techniques because with a little practice these can easily be acquired. The problem is that the gun's reservoir can only be filled with one shade of one colour at a time. With normal brushes you can, by picking up a little more or a little less of each colour with each dip of the brush, change tonal values, even hues can be adjusted with each new brushful. With an air brush the reservoir has to be emptied out (and possibly cleaned) and

Here the SIMAIR set-up is used with a Badger gun to apply an acrylic sealer.

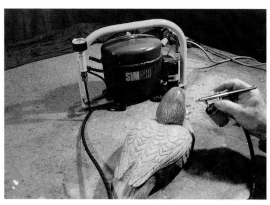

The head colour is built up.

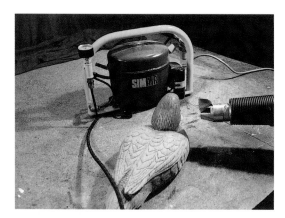

A layer of paint is dried with a hot-air gun.

The finished head and breast zone with a base brown applied to the flanks.

recharged with each change of shade. Actually, a lot can be done with only one change. The darkest shade is sprayed on over most of the area. The paint is changed to the lightest shade and this is then applied working slowly towards the darker, increasing the distance of the gun from the painted area as you reach the merge zone. This gives a mist overlay with a long merging zone where the tone slowly changes from light to dark.

Where using an air brush becomes extremely complicated and a considerable level of skill is required is where you have multi-banded colours on each feather. You will probably find it much easier to apply the body colour and main zones of highlight, shadow or colour variation using an air brush and then apply the detailing using techniques, brushes and strokes from the Featherstroke approach. Feather flicking still becomes one of the most important strokes in your repertoire.

There is little point here in recommending air compressor settings as each brush will have its own. Equally, as was stated a moment ago, some of the acrylic paints require dilution and again each make has its own dilution level. However, to give you some idea, I use a second-hand outfit acquired through an ad-mag. It consists of a Badger 100 brush (very much lower-middle end of the price range) with three different sizes of needle. It is recommended that it be used with the air pressure set at 30 PSI, but it will operate at anything between 15 to 50 PSI – of course the volume of air required is minuscule. My compressor is a Simair. Most of the paint I use should be diluted with equal volumes of water but, as I keep trying out different makes, I am not sure what it will be next week!

The fundamental skill in using an air brush is timing the triggering of the paint. The hand is always moving so the air is triggered as the sweep of the hand begins and the paint addition starts precisely as you reach the beginning of the colour zone. The paint is stopped at the end of the zone and then the air. Unless you are aiming for a gradual mist fade the brush must be kept at a constant distance from the surface. Too close and the air blast will push beads of paint out sideways (known as centipedes). If the paint looks grainy then you need to increase dilution. It took me four days of systematic practice before I got it anywhere near right. Eventually you will be in full control, and dots and fine straight lines will just flow from your 'brush'.

One imperative is that the gun is always kept absolutely clean. All traces of paint are removed while still wet. Nozzles should be cleaned out with the utmost

And a Cheeky Chappie to finish with. A Judith Nicoll Robin.

caution as they are easily damaged.

I have to say on balance that I would not bother. There are two reasons for saying this: it will take time before you get it right, and unless you are specifically interested in experimenting and trying out different things for the sake of variety then it is not worth the time investment. In the end you will achieve better results if you stick to paint and a selection of hair and bristle brushes.

And this leads directly to my final comments in the concluding chapter.

15

FAREWELL – VERY WELL!

I hope that this book has opened doors for you. I became very conscious early on that we might be opening too many doors and thereby causing confusion. Even in the last chapter you were presented with choices – twice! There was the choice between gessoing or lacquering, and the choice between conventional brushes or an air brush; even between highlights first or last.

That many choices can put some people off – they like to be given a single clear route map with precise instructions on how to walk it. Others, and hopefully you are amongst them, like to experiment. They are happier knowing that if one way does not work, then there are others where the end results will be similar. For different individuals some methods are themselves more satisfying than others.

I also specifically chose to follow a particular route with the illustrations. By using some pictures of Judith Nicoll's work it gave me the opportunity of showing you the ultimate possibilities. I am extremely grateful to Judith. She has long been an inspiration and a friend and although I sometimes have aspirations to do her type of work, I am broadly content to stay with my own pyrographed approach. I have therefore had to turn also to that brilliant colourist Jan Sanders for a supreme example of wood staining. Thanks to you, too, Jan.

A lot of my own recent feather-burnt work has been used to illustrate points of text, but you will also find something else. I still have some of my own, and some of my students' early work, so some of the illustrations are drawn from this source. These are constant reminders that we were all beginners at one time, and that everything does not always come 'just right'.

Many people when they see a pyrographed feather-burnt bird ask how I have the patience to do it. It is not really a question of patience. It is just that you adopt a different mind-set. First the activity itself is enormously satisfying – even the hours of pyro work. There is then the huge satisfaction of seeing the finished piece of work – a creation of your own hands that will cause people to exclaim with pleasure. (And the occasional sale and commission has lubricated more than one Christmas!)

A part of the mind-set is to welcome the opportunity that the burning activity provides. It is very nice to be able to switch not off, but out. You can not become actively involved in something else – not even thinking about that report that you have to write or whatever. Bird carving has two stages: one where it demands your full attention – while you are shaping the bird and working the detail – and the other where you can carry on with only part of the brain involved as, for example, during the 20 hours it may take to pyrograph the feathers. You obviously can not be actively involved in much else at this stage (other than gossiping), but there are many things in which you can become passively involved. I have enjoyed many radio plays and endless hours of wonderful music, including some magnificent operas, while carving birds.

Not a craft fair! A display of work in my studio when the garden was open as part of the village open day.

One thing is absolutely certain. There are few, if any, better ways of getting away from all the stresses and strains of the day – the whole pace of life changes when you sit down and know that for the next hour or two you have only this task in hand to concern yourself with.

As we said in an earlier chapter, you can take your interest just as far as you want to go. You can keep it as a very satisfying but gentle relaxation for an hour or two every so often by strictly focusing upon carving and decorating birds from bought, ready-shaped blanks. Or you can make it a lifetime's obsession becoming part twitcher, artist, photographer, wood-worker, carver and so on. I hope that you enjoy the thought of these many opportunities, even if you decide to accept only a limited part of them. My concern is that by even mentioning them, we may have frightened some people into thinking that the whole subject is too vast to contemplate. You can choose all, or only one specific part and you will still derive huge enjoyment and satisfaction from what you decide to do.

FURTHER READING

This is not intended to be an exhaustive review of all the books that might be of interest to the decoy carver/painter, but merely provides a few notes on some of the books that I have acquired over the years and found to be useful.

If you wish to extend your literature search you could do a lot worse than getting hold of the Stobart Davies book list – it is sectionalized and covers almost every area of woodwork. Stobarts are both publishers and booksellers.

GENERAL CARVING

Norbury, I., *Techniques of Creative Woodcarving* (Stobart, 1986) Ian Norbury is an English master carver. This book is good on equipment, a little thin on actual tool handing techniques but excellent on projects and laying out. It includes plans for a good chip-carved Falcon.

Norbury, I., *Projects for Creative Carving* (Stobart, 1986) The book includes many excellent smooth-finish and chip-carved projects amongst which are three birds.

Denning, A., *The Craft of Woodcarving* (Quatro, 1994) A nice little book – almost coffee-table presentation. Good on tools and tool handling, but no birds amongst the many excellent projects.

DECOY AND BIRD CARVING TECHNIQUES

Spielman, P., *Making Wood Decoys* (Stirling) An excellent introduction to techniques. Takes you step by step through the making of all types of decoys. Runs out of steam on painted realistic ducks and is spoilt by almost total use of black and white pictures that are poorly reproduced.

Bridgenhagen, K. and P. Spielman, *Realistic Decoys* (Stirling, 1984) Overlaps and then follows on from *Making Wood Decoys*. Good on detail and on finishing wood carved birds. Only a little use of colour pictures.

Ridges, B., *The Decoy Duck* (Dragons World, 1988) Looks at several of the top American carvers, using excellent colour pictures. Ends with a short but useful chapter on carving and painting.

Dehos, B. and P. Spielman, *Carving Large Birds* (Stirling) This book is for the chain-saw owner. It deals with the making of stylized wood-carved large birds in at least lifesize. There is not much on techniques but there are a number of scaled plans and abundant photo illustrations of points of detail for each project.

Schroder, R., *How to Carve Wildfowl* (Stackpole, 1984) This work comes in two hardback volumes and tends to be expensive if bought in the UK (So try the web!). They are wonderful but 'bitty'. Techniques are developed a chapter at a time by focusing upon the work of a different carver for each technique. The books are badly let down by the almost total use of black and white illustrations; this becomes ridiculous in the chapter on the work of Larry Hayden who paints carvings and pictures. 'Colour mixing' in black and white really is a waste of time.

PATTERN BOOKS

McGowan, P., *The Decorative Duck Design Book* (Old Hall Decoys). This is my favourite. There are 24 sets of plans each with plan, profile and section drawings. They are all lifesize although in one or two cases they are suspiciously close to the upper extreme. Feather layouts are clearly shown. A number of my successful early bird carvings came from this book.

Bridenhagen, K., *Decoy Pattern Book* (Sterling). Good plan and profile drawings of twenty-eight ducks. No sections but some detail illustration. Wing feathers detailed. The problem is that all drawings are 'Texas scale' and need to be scaled down by 15 to 20 per cent for realistic UK birds. Nevertheless useful.

Hillman, A., *Carving Water Birds*
Hillman, A., *Carving Birds of Prey*
Shrouds, H. and Hillman, A., *Carving Shorebirds*
Shrouds, H. and Hillman, A., *Carving Duck Decoys*
Shrouds, H. and Hillman, A., *Decorative Duck Decoys*
All Published by Dover.

These softback books come nearest to true working decoys. The ducks are shown full bodied for hollowing. Some of the birds in *Carving Water Birds* need scaling up and virtually no feather detailing is given – good for wood-carved birds. Almost all the twelve birds in *Carving Birds of Prey* need scaling. Most of the Decoys in *Carving Duck Decoys* are oversized and too simplistic; and obviously the American birds are better fed than are their smaller equivalents in the UK. *Carving Shorebirds* is good – here all the drawings are lifesized and all give enough detail to make good painted slicks.

Woodcarvers Favourite Patterns Book Series:
Carving 20 Realistic Game and Song Birds – Book 1
Realism in Wood – Book 2
Nature in Wood – Book 3
Carving Wildlife in Wood – Book 4
All by George Lehman and published by Fox Chapel.

This is an extremely good series with plan, profile and section drawings plus detail of heads, legs and specific points of interest. There are open-wing patterns showing all feathers and often instruction on making particular elements including the insertion of feathers. Many patterns are shown on detailed mounts and settings. They take you right up to the stage of being ready to paint, but do not go into this aspect. In all they provide a lifetime's supply of carving patterns – not all of which are birds.

Decorative Decoy Designs Series:
Volume 1: *Dabbling and Whistling Ducks*
Volume 2: *Diving Ducks*
Volume 3: *Geese and Swans*
All by Bruce Burk and published by Stackpole.

Superb full-scale profile and plan outlines with both line and colour feather layouts. The books can be used for slicks, but are primarily aimed at realistic birds. Some of the swan plans are scaled down, which is just as well as full-size swan plan books will not fit on the bookshelves!

Mohrhardt, D., *Encyclopaedia of Bird Reference Drawings* (Fox Chapel) This is not a pattern book but does provide useful extra detail to add to the drawings in the other books. There are spread-wing feather layouts, feet, beak, eye and tail details. It is part of the 'essential reference' list.

DECOY PAINTING

Hillman, A., *Painting Duck Decoys* (Dover, 1985) This is a worthwhile addition to the shelves. Twenty-four plates give plan and profile illustrations of twelve ducks. Each is painted in full colour and shows full feather layout suitable for Decorative Decoys (Slicks). There are also six pages of text suggesting colours to use.

Hopper, B., *Wildfowl Painting* (Martin Webber, 1985). Beebe Hopper developed and taught me a style of painting known as Feather Stroke. This book gives an insight into some of her techniques and then provides extremely good detailed instruction on the painting of six different birds. There is also guidance on doing a painting of birds. Essentially Beebe's technique is concerned with slicks although some bodies are surface textured.

Sprainkle, J.D., *Painting Waterfowl* (Stackpole, 1991) This is the most expensive book in my collection and is greatly treasured. It does, however, make you wish that it was a video – you want to see the brush travelling! Thirteen projects are detailed with multiple colour close-ups – every one a target of perfection to aim for. The results are complete works of art although sometimes you have a slight feeling that everything is 'too perfect'. Incredible as real ducks are, nature is rarely that precise. Again, buy it direct from the States!

SUPPLIERS

BOOKS

Stobart Davies, Priory House, 2 Priory Street, Hertford, SG14 1RN.

BIRD CARVERS' SUPPLIES (WOOD, TOOLS, BOOKS, FITTINGS, etc)

Pintail Carving, 20 Sheppenhall Grove, Nantwich, Cheshire CW5 8DF.

The Decoy Gallery, Hollow Marsh, Farrington Gurney, Bristol, BS18 5TX.

J. Lajevardi, 20A Lower Park Row, Bristol BS1 5BN.

TIMBER AND A WIDE RANGE OF TOOLS

Yandle and Sons Ltd, Hurst Works, Martock, Somerset TA12 6JU.

Lincolnshire Woodcraft Supplies, The Old Sawmill, Burghley Park, London Road, Wothorpe, Stamford, Lincs PE8 3JS (Good for Lime blocks).

TOOLS ONLY

Ashley Isles (Edge Tools) Ltd, East Kirkby, Spilsby, Lincolnshire OE23 4DD (and Rexon grinders).
Axminster Power Tools, Chard Street, Axminster, Devon EX13 5DZ.

POWER CARVING EQUIPMENT

Duplicarver, Arbortec and so on – Rod Naylor, 208 Devizes Road, Hilperton, Trowbridge, Wilts BA14 7QP.

Bourdet – Avery Knight and Bowles, James Street West, Bath, Avon BA1 2BT.

GLASS EYES

Eyedentity, The Manor House, Church Hill, Saxmundham, Suffolk IP17 1EU.

TAXIDERMIST

Kenny Everett, Two Hoots Taxidermy, 8 Trefusis Close, Truro, Cornwall TR1 1LJ.

INDEX